MW00476019

COMMUNION WITH CHRIST

COMMUNION WITH CHRIST

according to
Saint Teresa Benedicta
of the Cross

By Sister M. Regina van den Berg, F.S.G.M.

With a Foreword by Alice von Hildebrand

IGNATIUS PRESS   SAN FRANCISCO

Cover art by Rellie Luciano Liwag

Cover design by Riz Boncan Marsella

© 2015 by Ignatius Press, San Francisco
All rights reserved
ISBN 978-1-58617-951-9
Library of Congress Control Number 2014943999
Printed in the United States of America ∞

CONTENTS

FOREWORD

Edith Stein—now Saint Edith Stein—was born on October 12, 1891, on the Jewish Day of Atonement, Yom Kippur; entered the Church shortly after her thirtieth birthday; and was murdered in Auschwitz in 1942, a few months after her fiftieth birthday. Her life as a Catholic was short, and her life as a Carmelite nun still shorter: she entered the blessed ark in 1933. Nine years later, all that remained of her body, sanctified and nourished by the Eucharist since her conversion, was a handful of dust.

Now she is known the world over, and innumerable people benefit not only from her writings, but most of all from her holiness. From the moment she was baptized, her life was characterized by her ardent desire to be united to the One Whom she now acknowledged to be the Savior of the world, the King of the Jews.

Many books have been written about her. Can a new book make significant new contributions? Without a moment's hesitation I claim that it can, and for the following reason: every saint shares with us a loving message of such depth that no one work can exhaust the treasures hidden in striving for holiness. Moreover, each loving admirer of a saint will inevitably direct our attention to certain facets of that saint's life and personality that have particularly enriched his own spiritual life. This is

7

clearly the case for Sister M. Regina. Saint Edith's message is not, as people like to say, "ahead of her time" (a very equivocal statement) but is above her time. Truth is timeless. This is why Saint Augustine's message is still very much alive today; the one of Heidegger and Sartre is fading fast.

Sister M. Regina is well qualified to write such a book. Having read much literature on the life and writings of this heroic victim of Nazism, she knows her topic; moreover, one feels that she not only loves her subject (can one understand a person for whom one has no sympathy—should I say empathy—?) but clearly regards Saint Edith as a role model, and this is "existentially" felt throughout her book.

The book is made up of six chapters. Each one deserves a careful analysis. I will limit myself to consider some key ideas because they center on questions that are and always will be of burning interest: the metaphysical situation of man both as a creature, totally dependent upon his Creator, and as a mysterious person, composed not only of soul and body but also of two genders, which, while complementary, are of equal dignity.

Apart from the abysmal divide separating God from all His creatures, there is a chasm separating persons and nonpersons. To say that a monkey is closer to a rock or a plant than to the human person is likely to arouse the intellectual ire of many of our contemporaries who eloquently try to convince us that man is just a more highly developed chimpanzee: the difference separating them being one of degree, not of nature. Yet we stand on firm ground by adopting the position of Saint Bonaventure, who wrote in his *Itinerarium mentis in Deum* that all material creatures are only "traces" of God (*vestigia*). Man alone is made to God's image (*imago*).

While studying at the University of Breslau, Edith was attracted to feminism; her strong sense of justice made her revolt against the denigration of the female sex as intellectually inferior. She was conscious that many of her male costudents were not on her level. She always achieved the highest grades. She did not hesitate to proclaim that she would not dream of giving up a challenging career for the sake of devoting herself to menial tasks in the narrow framework of the life of a married woman.

No one can go wrong in combating injustice, but one must have the right motivation. The problem with many types of feminism is that their "mothers" have totally lost sight of the beauty of femininity. Simone de Beauvoir wrote bluntly: "Women hate being women. They dislike their bodies." This famous "mother" of French feminism is, I fear, willfully blind to the glorious role assigned to woman in the Old Testament. Not only is hers the only body made from the body of a person, but, moreover, as revealed in the New Testament, there is only one person, a female, who was created without the stain of Original Sin. This woman, who is *tota pulchra*, was found worthy to become the Mother of the Savior, who has no earthly father. It is a woman, not a man, who is above angels: *Regina Angelorum*. Feminists are cursed by blindness.

The day Edith entered the Church, her eyes were opened, and she clearly knew she had the mission of reopening women's eyes to the beauty of the vocation of womanhood.

All "revolutionary" causes need a valid "justification". Alas, too often this legitimate recrimination is poisoned by other factors, which instead of remedying an unjust situation create problems of equal, if not greater, magnitude. Edith, as a teenager, had abandoned her Jewish faith but not her ardent longing to find truth. This was the golden thread that led her to the one true Faith in the Catholic Church. Not only did her truth-thirsting soul immediately perceive and accept Christ—a Jew—as the Savior of the world, but the message was meaningfully communicated to her through a woman, one of the greatest saints of our Holy Church, Saint Teresa of Avila. Clearly God's providence was at work. Edith spent a whole night reading the autobiography of this great mystic. It was clear to her, upon closing the book, that the Catholic Church had the fullness of truth, and her decision to become a child of the Church was immediate and irrevocable. She heard the call and immediately responded: "I am the handmaid of the Lord." She wanted to devote her life to the Bride of her Savior. Her vocation was born with her faith. This decision was not the fruit of a short-lived enthusiasm; it was a response to grace. What she had perceived was so luminous, so convincing, had so clearly the taste of the supernatural, that no further search was necessary. She bought herself a catechism, studied Catholic doctrine, and very soon was ready for baptism. With her brilliant intelligence and her loving heart opened to truth, she was ready for this great sacrament.

One thing is clear: the moment she had found the fullness of truth, she was going to live it and to strive to attain holiness; her ascension on the Holy Mount was her one and only desire. She never did things halfway: she became a daily communicant from the day of her baptism and devoted time to prayer and meditation. But she also realized she needed help and guidance. Saint Teresa taught her that spiritual guidance is crucial when striving for holiness. How easily we can imagine that our wishes are God's will for us. Edith had an iron will. She came close to a nervous breakdown when, shortly after going to Göttingen, where the intellectual level was much higher than in Breslau, she had to acknowledge that, to her amazement, she could no longer achieve brilliant results by "sheer will power". If this applied to her intellectual pursuits, it applied a fortiori to the science of the cross.

She immediately looked for a spiritual director and found one in the person of Father Joseph Schwind. Upon his death, she looked for another spiritual guide and asked a Benedictine monk, Archabbot Raphael Walzer, to accept her as his spiritual daughter. She decided to submit her will to his advice. Had she not promised her Savior, the moment she found Him, that she would give Him everything? Christ requested not only her heart but also her will. Clearly the convent was the classical road to holiness, where one is bound by a vow of obedience. Edith wanted to become a Carmelite nun. But her spiritual guide opposed her wishes, and even though obedience did not come easily to her, as Sister M. Regina underlines, she commanded her will and made the discovery that submission is not weakness but strength. She also realized that, ardent as her desire was to give up everything to buy the pearl of great price, she could not impose a second blow on her beloved mother, who was already shattered by her conversion.

Following her spiritual director's advice, she accepted a teaching position in a school in Speyer. She, the brilliant student of Edmund Husserl, who had received her doctorate summa cum laude, knew that universities were not open to women. She humbly followed the advice of her director and taught for eight years in Speyer. Later, also upon his recommendation, she started to give talks not only in Germany but in other countries as well. All this was done under strict obedience and, at times, very much against her own wishes and desires. "Not my will, but Thy will be done."

But her longing to enter Carmel was still alive in her soul. She was convinced that she had a vocation but waited patiently for the *placet* of Dom Walzer. However, when the Nazi poison made her work impossible, she once again expressed her desire to become a Carmelite nun. Dom Walzer finally gave her permission to follow the longing of her heart, sacrificed for many years. Without his permission, she would not have knocked on the door of the Carmel in Cologne. She wanted her most ardent wish to be "baptized" by an act of obedience. To give everything to God means essentially to give Him both our heart and our will.

Now that she had learned by practice the spiritual treasure of "dying to oneself", she was ready to share it with others. Her students in Speyer were aware that she spent long hours in front of the Blessed Sacrament, and they inevitably turned to her for help and advice. She did not seek to guide others; she did so only when it became clear to her that God wanted her to do so. She warned one of her spiritual protégées that it was dangerous to adhere to her "obstinate self-will ... a tenacious clinging to her desires once conceived". To love another person is to be ardently concerned about his spiritual health and to fight relentlessly against the obstacles that prevent him from becoming "free" for God.

We saw the key role that Saint Teresa of Avila played in Edith's conversion in the course of a single night. After her conversion, Edith was inevitably challenged to reexamine her views on womanhood. How could she miss the luminous message given her through a female creature such as Saint Teresa, sharing the very same sex, who had achieved spiritual greatness through humility and love? Not only is Mary the beloved of God, but she also is the mother par excellence. She is indeed the Mother of the only Priest: her Son.

How could someone who had abandoned her faith, such as Simone de Beauvoir, understand the mystery of femininity? Clearly the brilliant student of Husserl could never have written so profoundly on masculinity and femininity before she was blessed with the Catholic teaching on the one called *tota pulchra*. It was an eye-opener for her, and her beautiful lines on the woman's understanding of "person" were clearly a fruit of her faith. Woman's vocation is to be the handmaid of the Lord—that is, to serve Him wherever He calls her.

Maybe her teaching could be summarized by quoting Dietrich von Hildebrand, who, in many of his talks, asked: What is the *thema Christi*? The *thema Christi*—that is, the particular task to which God calls a person at this particular moment—is the best way of glorifying God and the surest way to holiness.

For a woman whose children are crying for her love and presence, the *thema Christi* is to attend to her children. What good would it do the woman to give a brilliant lecture while ignoring the tears of her children? This "holy flexibility"— the fruit of lovingly embracing the cross—was a blessed art that Edith mastered and which reveals the golden thread that led her to Auschwitz.

The talk that Edith delivered in Salzburg in 1930 was a typical example of the fecundating effect that faith has on reason. How could secular feminism compete with the glorious mission that the Church has assigned to the "weak" sex? The way Edith expounds and develops the complementariness of man and woman and the way they mutually enrich one another is remarkable. Her faith had fecundated her reason and made her conscious of the fact that a person's full and loving acceptance of the sex God has chosen for him will enable him to understand "the other sex". On the other hand, no one is capable of truly understanding the beauty and mission of the sex God has chosen for him when his spiritual eyesight has been blinded by secular philosophy. Man's greatness is achieved not through exterior feats (inventions, fame, money, power) but by fulfilling his God-given calling. The saintly woman is the one who truly understands the beauty and mission of femininity, not as a head of state or as a virago aiming at dominating others, but as *ancilla Domini*, as Mary has taught us. It was in light of such an understanding that holy and perfectly chaste friendships between members of the opposite sex have enabled numerous saints throughout the ages to fulfill their God-given mission. One thinks of the

Blessed Virgin Mary and Saint Joseph, Saint Francis of Assisi and Saint Clare, Saint Teresa of Avila and Saint John of the Cross, and Saint Francis de Sales and Saint Jane Frances de Chantal.

Service is the road to freedom. Richly endowed with intellectual gifts that God had placed in her cradle, Edith also had a strong will, and she acknowledges that, even as a very young girl, she was indomitable. Moreover, she knew how to assert her will and to armor herself when she was imposed upon by her mother or her siblings. It is not by accident that—as testified by the history of the Church—some of the greatest saints who were also endowed with a strong will were precisely those who achieved the heights of holiness by submitting joyfully and totally to the will of God. This is why a vow of obedience is required in religious orders. Sister M. Regina makes it clear that Edith's spiritual ear was always attuned to God's commands. This gives us a key to her martyrdom and her holiness. This book is invaluable for women who have lost sight of the sublimity of their mission. *Tolle lege.*

Dr. Alice von Hildebrand
Memorial of Saint Teresa Benedicta of the Cross
August 9, 2014
New Rochelle, New York

ACKNOWLEDGMENT

The present book has its origin in the early months of 2003, when Raymond Leo Cardinal Burke, then bishop of La Crosse, Wisconsin, invited me to offer a series of talks about Saint Teresa Benedicta of the Cross. At the encouragement of Mother M. Ingeborg Rohner, F.S.G.M., my Provincial Superior at the time, I gave a series of six talks titled "Becoming One Heart and One Soul" during Lent of 2003 at the Shrine of Our Lady of Guadalupe in La Crosse. I express my deepest gratitude to His Eminence and to Mother M. Ingeborg for their support in preparing the talks that gave rise to *Communion with Christ according to Saint Teresa Benedicta of the Cross*.

Sister M. Regina van den Berg, F.S.G.M.
December 8, 2014
Solemnity of the Immaculate Conception
of the Blessed Virgin Mary

INTRODUCTION

In his Apostolic Letter *Novo Millennio Ineunte*, written at the conclusion of the Great Jubilee Year 2000, Pope Saint John Paul II drew up what he called a "post-Jubilee pastoral plan"[1] for the Church in the new millennium. In the fourth chapter, he declares that the great challenge of the new millennium is to make the Church *"the home and school of communion"*.[2] Communion, John Paul II explains, "is the fruit and demonstration of that love which springs from the heart of the Eternal Father and is poured out upon us through the Spirit which Jesus gives us (cf. Rom 5:5), to make us all 'one heart and one soul' (Acts 4:32)".[3] John Paul II explains that communion cannot be achieved through a practical plan or program, but rather we *"need to promote a spirituality of communion"*.[4] He outlines four aspects of such a spirituality:

1. It "indicates above all the heart's contemplation of the mystery of the Trinity dwelling in us,... whose light we must be able to see shining on the face of the brothers and sisters around us."

---

[1] John Paul II, Apostolic Letter *Novo Millennio Ineunte* (Boston: Pauline Books and Media, 2001), no. 15.
[2] Ibid., no. 43.
[3] Ibid., no. 42.
[4] Ibid., no. 43.

2. It "also means an ability to think of our brothers and sisters in faith with the profound unity of the Mystical Body, and therefore as 'those who are a part of me'."

3. It "implies also the ability to see what is positive in others, to welcome it and prize it as a gift from God."

4. It "means, finally, to know how to 'make room' for our brothers and sisters ... resisting the selfish temptations which constantly beset us and provoke competition, careerism, distrust, and jealousy."[5]

The word *communion* has two distinct but related meanings, as Father Louis Bouyer clarifies in his *Dictionary of Theology*: "The first designates the participation of the faithful in the Eucharist through the eating of the consecrated species. The second, which may be more aptly expressed by the word *fellowship*, refers to the community life in the Mystical Body of Christ that is the effect of the Eucharist."[6] It is primarily this second meaning of *communion* that Pope Saint John Paul II intends in the above-mentioned passages of *Novo Millenio Ineunte*. Since our union with Christ, the Head of the Mystical Body, is most profound when

---

[5] Ibid.

[6] Louis Bouyer, *Dictionary of Theology*, trans. Charles Underhill Quinn (New York: Desclee, 1965), p. 91, s.v. "Communion". Cf. *Catechism of the Catholic Church* (*CCC*), 2nd ed. (Washington, D.C.: Libreria Editrice Vaticana, 2000), p. 871, s.v. "communion": "Holy Communion, the reception of the Body and Blood of Christ in the Eucharist (1382). More generally, our fellowship and union with Jesus and other baptized Christians in the Church, which has its source and summit in the celebration of the Eucharist. In this sense, the Church as communion is the deepest vocation of the Church (959)."

we receive Holy Communion, the first sense of the term is both the source and the summit of the second sense of the word.

A spirituality of communion finds its expression in being united in thinking and willing, in sharing a common end, and in tending toward that end in common as "we". The end toward which the members of the Mystical Body tend is the highest possible end, namely, the salvation of each soul and the glory of God Himself. Pope Venerable Pius XII expressed it in his Encyclical Letter *Mystici Corporis Christi* as follows:

> Our union in and with Christ is first evident from the fact that, since Christ wills His Christian community to be a Body which is a perfect Society, its members must be united because they all work together towards a single end. The nobler the end towards which they strive, and the more divine the motive which actuates this collaboration, the higher, no doubt, will be the union. Now the end in question is supremely exalted; the continual sanctifying of the members of the Body for the glory of God and of the Lamb that was slain.[7]

Pope Pius XII further explains that the union in the Mystical Body "is supplemented by another internal principle, which exists effectively in the whole and in each of its parts, and whose excellence is such that of itself it is vastly superior to whatever bonds of union may be found in a physical or

[7] Pius XII, Encyclical Letter *Mystici Corporus Christi* [*On the Mystical Body of Christ*] (Vatican City State: Libreria Editrice Vaticana, 1943), no. 68.

moral body.... This is something not of the natural but of the supernatural order...: the Spirit of God."[8] In the Mystical Body, then, members are united not only by a common tending toward a goal, but also and primarily by the Spirit of God.

The spirituality of communion is a spirituality of mutual charity, but, as Pope Benedict XVI expressed it in his Encyclical Letter *Caritas in Veritate*: "*Only in truth does charity shine forth*, only in truth can charity be authentically lived."[9] It is only when human persons live in truth that they can be united in community: "*Truth*, in fact, is *logos* which creates *diá-logos*, and hence communication and communion."[10]

Although she died about a generation ago and never heard Pope John Paul II's call to foster a spirituality of communion, Edith Stein can help us to meet the challenge to communion. Edith Stein was a Jew who became a philosopher; she was a convert to Catholicism who became a Carmelite nun and crowned her life with martyrdom. As a Carmelite, she took the name Sister Teresa Benedicta of the Cross, in honor of Saint Teresa of Jesus, the great reformer of the Carmelite Order, and in honor of the Cross of Christ. Edith Stein's writings provide insights that can help us to grow in the spirituality of communion, first, by presenting to us the truth about the human person's nature and vocation and then by

[8] Ibid., no. 62.
[9] Benedict XVI, Encyclical Letter *Caritas in Veritate* [*Charity in Truth*] (Vatican City State: Libreria Editrice Vaticana, 2009), no. 3.
[10] Ibid., no. 4.

showing how we can arrive at a spirituality of communion in the various aspects of life.[11]

In the first chapter, we will consider our communion with Christ, especially with His Cross. The second chapter reflects upon the importance of empathy in establishing communion with our brothers and sisters. Edith Stein emphasized that men and women have distinct roles and vocations, and the third chapter addresses communion between men and women. One aspect of our communion with God is our responding to His particular will for us, and so the fourth chapter considers our vocations and daily lives. The spirituality of communion, according to Pope Saint John Paul II, is to be the guiding principle of education; thus, the fifth chapter considers the implications of this proposition. The final chapter examines Edith Stein's studies on how community life can assist us in our efforts to make our communities homes of communion.

[11] Throughout the text, I have used the name Edith Stein when referring to or quoting from her as a laywoman and the name Sister Teresa Benedicta when referring to or quoting from her as a Carmelite nun.

I

Communion with Christ and His Cross

The sacraments are the primary means for entering into communion with Christ and His Church. Through baptism, we enter into Christ's death, are buried with Him, and rise with Him.[1] Baptism brings us into the Church, the Mystical Body of Christ. In the Holy Eucharist, our union with Christ is especially profound, and it is for this reason called *Holy* Communion. We think also of the sacrament of penance, in which we come to Christ after we have damaged or broken our communion with Him. Through the ministry of the priest, Christ absolves us of our sins so that we can, once again, live in harmony with Him.

The Christ to whom we seek to be united chose to redeem us by His suffering and death on the Cross. If we seek communion with a suffering Savior, we, too, must share in His suffering in some way. If Christ the Head suffers, we, His body, must also do so.

Like each of us, Saint Teresa Benedicta of the Cross encountered suffering in her life, and she learned to value

[1] See *CCC* 1227.

her suffering greatly since it was both a sign and a means of
union with the crucified Lord. We begin, then, by looking
at her life in order to see the prominence of the cross, so that
we can consider how she learned to live in union with her
suffering Savior.

The Cross in Edith Stein's Life

Edith Stein was born into a practicing Jewish family in Breslau, Germany, on the Jewish Day of Atonement, October 12, 1891. Jews observe this most solemn day of the Jewish
year by a rigorous twenty-four-hour fast from food and drink
and by nearly uninterrupted prayer in the synagogue. Should
we think the Jewish fast difficult to keep, Edith Stein assures
us that we are not alone. We read in her autobiography that
her sister Frieda never rose from bed on the Day of Atonement, because if she did, she would have been unable to keep
the fast.[2] On this solemn day, Jews beg God's forgiveness for
all their sins. At the synagogue the rabbi prays: "From this
day shall be made an atonement for you to cleanse you that
you may be clean from all your sins before the Lord."[3] At the
end of the fast, a horn is blown to announce a new birth from

[2] See *The Collected Works of Edith Stein*, vol. 1, *Life in a Jewish Family (1891–
1916)*, trans. Sister Josephine Koeppel, O.C.D., ed. L. Gelber and R. Leuven,
O.C.D. (Washington, D.C.: ICS Publications, 1986), p. 72.

[3] *The Form of Daily Prayers* (Frankfurt am Main: J. Kauffmann, 1876),
pp. 327–28, in Freda Mary Oben, *The Life and Thought of St. Edith Stein* (New
York: Alba House, 2001), p. 5.

sin into freedom. The Day of Atonement reminds Christians of Christ, the Paschal Lamb who died for our sins. Edith Stein's birth on this day already associates her with the cross.

Although her family practiced the Jewish faith, at the age of fourteen Edith Stein deliberately decided to cease praying.[4] She did not stop praying because she was a rebellious teenager, but because she was earnestly and painfully seeking the truth and did not find it in her Jewish faith. As a university student, she searched for the truth in her studies, first at Breslau University, later at Göttingen University. Looking back later on these years, Edith writes, "My longing for truth was itself a prayer."[5]

As a student of philosophy at Göttingen, Edith first encountered and later embraced the Catholic Faith. She was introduced to Max Scheler, a Jewish convert to Catholicism, who gave unofficial lectures at Göttingen. For the first time, Edith had met someone who intelligently combined faith and reason. She writes of Max Scheler's lectures: "This was my first encounter with this hitherto totally unknown world. It did not lead me as yet to the Faith. But it did open for me a region of 'phenomena' which I could then no longer bypass blindly."[6]

Although she does not write much about the reasons for her conversion to Catholicism, she does mention that she was deeply moved by the witness of Anna Reinach, a Jewish

---

[4] See Stein, *Life in a Jewish Family*, p. 148.

[5] Quoted in Sister Teresia Renata Posselt, O.C.D., *Edith Stein: The Life of a Philosopher and Carmelite*, ed. Susanne M. Batzdorff, Sister Josephine Koeppel, O.C.D., and Reverend John Sullivan, O.C.D. (Washington, D.C.: ICS Publications, 2005), p. 63.

[6] Stein, *Life in a Jewish Family*, p. 260.

woman who, with her husband, had converted to Christianity in 1916.[7] Her husband, Adolf Reinach, was one of Edith Stein's professors at Göttingen. During World War I, Professor Reinach served his country and fell in battle in 1917. Mrs. Reinach asked Edith to put into order her deceased husband's papers. When Edith met the recently widowed Mrs. Reinach, she was astounded to discover that she was not a bitter and broken woman, but that she was embracing the cross. She writes: "It was my first encounter with the Cross and the divine power that it bestows on those who carry it. For the first time, I was seeing with my very eyes the Church, born from her Redeemer's suffering, triumphant over the sting of death. That was the moment my unbelief collapsed and Christ shone forth—in the mystery of the Cross."[8] It appears that Edith had been struggling with the problem of evil and that Mrs. Reinach's faith gave her a glimpse of the solution to the mystery.

There are other events that contributed to Edith's conversion. She tells us how moved she was when she saw a woman with a shopping basket enter a Catholic church to make a visit. It was, she said, as though the woman were going to have an

---

[7] Both Anna Reinach and her sister-in-law Pauline Reinach later converted to Catholicism. Pauline became a Benedictine nun (see Stein, *Life in a Jewish Family*, p. 496, n. 142).

[8] Quoted in Teresia Renata Posselt, *Edith Stein: Eine Grosse Frau unseres Jahrhunderts*, 9th ed. (Freiburg-Basel-Vienna: Herder, 1963), p. 49. English translation in Waltraud Herbstrith, *Edith Stein: A Biography*, trans. Father Bernard Bonowitz, O.C.S.O., 2nd ed. (San Francisco: Ignatius Press, 1992), p. 56. For a slightly different English translation, see Posselt, *Edith Stein: The Life of a Philosopher and Carmelite*, p. 59.

intimate conversation with someone. She had never seen any-thing like this; she had been to churches only for services.[9] Like Mrs. Reinach, the woman who made the visit impressed Edith, it seems, because the woman's faith informed her daily life; her faith was a communion with a Person.

Edith's actual conversion to the Catholic Faith, prepared by these events, was occasioned by reading the autobiography of Saint Teresa of Jesus, *The Book of Her Life*, while visiting her friends the Conrad-Martiuses at their home. Having finished the book, Edith knew, "That is the truth!"[10] and immedi-ately purchased a missal and a catechism. After studying these books, she was baptized on January 1, 1922, at the age of thirty-one, taking Theresia Hedwig as her baptismal name.

From the outset, the Catholic Faith and the cross were wedded for Edith Stein. Once baptized, she had to tell her mother. Her Jewish mother did not understand her conver-sion and felt as though she had lost her daughter. It is not difficult to imagine the deep suffering this misunderstanding caused both mother and daughter. Some time later, Edith wrote to one of her students: "If you have not yet expe-rienced it, you will realize it later: it is one of the greatest

[9] See Stein, *Life in a Jewish Family*, p. 401: "But the deepest impressions were made on me by things other than the Römerweg and the Hirschgraben. We stopped in at the cathedral for a few minutes; and, while we looked around in the respectful silence, a woman carrying a market basket came in and knelt down in one of the pews to pray briefly. This was something entirely new to me. To the synagogues or to the Protestant churches which I had visited, one went only for services. But here was someone interrupting her everyday shop-ping errands to come into this church, although no other person was in it, as though she were here for an intimate conversation. I could never forget that."

[10] Quoted in Posselt, *Edith Stein: The Life of a Philosopher and Carmelite*, p. 63.

sorrows in life to be interiorly separated from those one loves, because they can no longer follow one. But such sorrow is also very fruitful."[11]

In addition to the exterior sufferings occasioned by her conversion, Edith also seems to have suffered in her spiritual life. There are times when we find no consolation in prayer and when it seems experientially that God is far from us. In 1931, Edith wrote an essay about Christmas. The tone of the essay suggests that she was no stranger to the spiritual sufferings she describes:

> In the infancy of the spiritual life, when we have just begun to surrender ourselves to God's guidance, we will feel His guiding hand very strongly: it is as clear as daylight what we have to do and what to avoid. But it will not always remain like this. He who belongs to Christ must live the whole Christ-life. He must mature into Christ's manhood; he must one day begin the Way of the Cross to Gethsemane and to Golgotha. And all the sufferings that can come from without are as nothing compared with the dark night of the soul, when the divine light no longer shines, and the voice of the Lord no longer speaks. God is there, but He is hidden and silent. Why is this so? We speak of the mysteries of God, which cannot be completely penetrated.[12]

---

[11] Quoted in Hilda C. Graef, *The Scholar and the Cross: The Life and Work of Edith Stein* (Maryland: The Newman Press, 1955), p. 38.

[12] Edith Stein, "Das Weihnachtsgeheimnis: Menschwerdung und Menschheit", in *Edith Steins Werke*, vol. 12, *Ganzheitliches Leben: Schriften zur religiösen Bildung* (Freiburg: Herder, 1990), p. 203. All translations of texts from *Ganzheitliches Leben* by Sister M. Regina van den Berg, F.S.G.M.

Once she had converted to the Faith, Edith desired to become a Carmelite, but, following the counsel of her spiritual director, she taught at a Dominican teachers' training college in Speyer. In 1932, she began to travel extensively, giving lectures on the role of women in society, methods of education, and the formation of children. She also became a lecturer at the Institute for Pedagogy at Münster, but, because of anti-Semitic legislation passed by the Nazi government, she was forced to resign the position the following year. Again, the cross appeared prominent in Edith's life.

Since Edith was unable to practice an active apostolate after the anti-Semitic legislation passed in 1933, her spiritual director no longer opposed her entrance to Carmel. Perhaps, too, since it had already been ten years since her conversion, Edith thought that her decision would be a little easier for her mother to accept. It was not. Before entering Carmel, she went home for a final visit. In September, a month before her entrance, Edith told her mother of her intention to enter Carmel. She describes the last night at home, writing of her mother: "She covered her face with her hands and began to weep. I stood behind her chair and held her silvery head to my breast. Thus we remained for a long while, until she let me persuade her to go to bed. I took her upstairs and helped her undress, for the first time in my life. Then I sat on the edge of her bed till she herself sent me to bed.... I don't think either of us found any rest that night."[13]

---

[13] Edith Stein, "How I Came to the Cologne Carmel", in Posselt, *Edith Stein: The Life of a Philosopher and Carmelite*, p. 128.

On October 14, 1933, the vigil of the feast of Saint Teresa of Jesus, having just turned forty-two, Edith entered Carmel. At the end of 1932, she had written to a former pupil about the Carmelite vocation:

There is a vocation to suffer with Christ and thereby to cooperate with him in his work of salvation. When we are united with the Lord, we are members of the mystical body of Christ: Christ lives on his members and continues to suffer in them. And the suffering borne in union with the Lord is his suffering, incorporated in the great work of salvation and fruitful therein. That is a fundamental premise of all religious life, above all of the life of Carmel, to stand proxy for sinners through voluntary and joyous suffering, and to cooperate in the salvation of humankind.[14]

Although she was filled with deep joy to be able to embrace, at last, the vocation to which she had felt called since her baptism, it must also have been difficult at her age to adjust to life at Carmel.[15]

[14] Stein to Annelies Lichtenberger, December 26, 1932, in *The Collected Works of Edith Stein*, vol. 5, *Edith Stein: Self-Portrait in Letters*, trans. Sister Josephine Koeppel, O.C.D., ed. L. Gelber and R. Leuven, O.C.D. (Washington, D.C.: ICS Publications, 1993), no. 129, p. 128.

[15] Cf. *Kölner Selig- und Heiligsprechungsprozess der Dienerin Gottes Sr. Teresia Benedicta a Cruce (Edith Stein): Professe und Chorschwester des Ordens der Allerseligsten Jungfrau Maria vom Berge Karmel* (Cologne: Kloster der Karmelitinnen "Maria vom Frieden", 1962), p. 79, no. 103: "A fellow novice reports about a conversation they had during recreation. The Sister in question had entered at a very young age, and one day she told the Servant of God how difficult it had been for her to adjust to the austerity of Carmel at such a young age. The Servant of God then responded, 'Yes, I understand that very well. But it is not easy either to adjust to Carmel at a mature age, at 40. They are

In a letter explaining her new religious name, which she received at her clothing six months after her entrance, Sister Teresa Benedicta of the Cross writes:

> I must tell you that I already brought my religious name with me into the house as a postulant. I received it exactly as I requested it. By the cross I understand the destiny of God's people which, even at that time, began to announce itself. I thought that those who recognized it as the cross of Christ had to take it upon themselves in the name of all. Certainly, today I know more of what it means to be wedded to the Lord in the sign of the Cross. Of course, one can never comprehend it, for it is a mystery.[16]

Sister Teresa Benedicta's mother was never reconciled with her daughter's vocation. Even in her final illness, her mother was "constantly brooding, wondering why her youngest has 'forsaken' her".[17] Her mother died on the feast of the Exaltation of the Holy Cross in 1936, the day that Sister Teresa Benedicta of the Cross renewed her vows.

After Sister Teresa Benedicta had spent four years in the Carmelite cloister in Cologne, the Nazi threat became ever

---

not the same difficulties one has when one is 20 years old, but they are no less difficult.'" All translations from *Kölner Selig- und Heiligsprechungsprozess der Dienerin Gottes Sr. Teresia Benedicta a Cruce (Edith Stein): Professe und Chorschwester des Ordens der Allerseligsten Jungfrau Maria vom Berge Karmel* by Sister M. Regina van den Berg, F.S.G.M. Cf. Herbstrith, *Edith Stein*, pp. 124ff.

[16] Sister Teresa Benedicta to Mother Petra Brüning, O.S.U., December 9, 1938, in Stein, *Self-Portrait in Letters*, no. 287, p. 295.

[17] Sister Teresa Benedicta to Hedwig Conrad-Martius, August 20, 1936, in ibid., no. 224, p. 233.

more alarming. Fearing that her presence as a Jew would endanger the safety of her community, Sister Teresa Benedicta asked to be transferred to another cloister.[18] Her move to the cloister of Echt, Netherlands, took place at the end of 1938. This transfer was not easy for her; once more, she was called to embrace the cross. In her letters, Sister Teresa Benedicta refers again and again to the difficulty of leaving her religious family in Cologne. To an acquaintance she writes, "You can imagine how very painful it was to leave Cologne."[19]

Once in Echt, she realized that she was again in danger and posed a threat to her sisters; therefore, she inquired about the possibility of being transferred to the Carmel of Le Pâquier, near Fribourg, Switzerland.[20] Writing to her superior about the proposed transfer, she says, "I am satisfied with everything. A *scientia crucis* [knowledge of the cross] can be gained only when one comes to feel the Cross radically. I have been convinced of that from the first moment and have said, from my heart: *Ave, Crux, spes unica!*"[21]

---

[18] Cf. Posselt, *Edith Stein: The Life of A Philosopher and Carmelite*, p. 181: "It was only natural that in Sr. Benedicta's own mind the thought of emigrating should arise, especially when she heard of people being harassed on account of their association with Jews. This made her fear for the beloved Carmelite family to which she belonged." Cf. ibid., p. 183: "When Sr. Benedicta learned all that had happened, she again proposed a transfer. Most of all she would have wished to go to Palestine to the Carmel in Bethlehem that a lay-Sister named Miriam (Mary) of Jesus Crucified, a great servant of God, had founded."

[19] Sister Teresa Benedicta to Anni Greven, January 14, 1939, in Stein, *Self-Portrait in Letters*, no. 292, p. 300.

[20] See Posselt, *Edith Stein: The Life of a Philosopher and Carmelite*, p. 196.

[21] Sister Teresa Benedicta to Mother Ambrosia Antonia Engelmann, O.C.D., December 1941, in Stein, *Self-Portrait in Letters*, no. 330, p. 341.

While the superiors were awaiting the final exit permits that would have allowed both Sister Teresa Benedicta and her sister Rosa to transfer to Switzerland, the premonition of Sister Teresa Benedicta came to pass.[22] On July 27, 1942, the Nazi leadership in occupied Holland ordered the deportation of all Roman Catholic Jews living in the Netherlands. Sister Teresa Benedicta and her sister Rosa, who had also converted to Catholicism and had become a Third Order Carmelite at the Carmel in Echt, were arrested. Along with many other Catholic Jews, including priests, religious, and laypeople, they were transported to the concentration camp at Auschwitz, where Sister Teresa Benedicta was sent to the gas chamber, probably on August 9, 1942.[23] From her birth on the Day of Atonement to her death as a martyr for the Catholic Faith, the life of Saint Teresa Benedicta of the Cross was signed by the cross.

The Spirituality of the Cross

Like Edith Stein, each of us experiences suffering—physical, mental, or spiritual. The presence of the cross in Saint Teresa Benedicta's life is not what sets her apart. What commands our attention is her attitude toward the crosses in her life.

[22] See Posselt, *Edith Stein: The Life of a Philosopher and Carmelite*, pp. 196ff., especially p. 207.

[23] For an extensive account of the events surrounding the arrest on July 2, 1942, and the internment and transport to Auschwitz, see Father Paul Hamans, *Edith Stein and Companions: On the Way to Auschwitz*, trans. Sister M. Regina van den Berg, F.S.G.M. (San Francisco: Ignatius Press, 2010), especially chapters 1 and 2.

Having learned to love Jesus Christ, Sister Teresa Benedicta recognized in all the sufferings of her life a means of
sharing His burden. The crosses of everyday life are the very
means by which our communion with Christ is established.
What is more, when we unite our sufferings to Christ's, we
make reparation for our sins and those of others and assist in
Christ's work of redemption. In an essay composed for her
sisters in Carmel, Sister Teresa Benedicta writes: "Everyone
who, in the course of time, has borne an onerous destiny
in remembrance of the suffering Savior or who has freely
taken up works of expiation has by so doing canceled some of
the mighty load of human sin and has helped the Lord carry
his burden."[24]

Sister Teresa Benedicta's philosophical background also
prepared her to understand how our sufferings can unite us
to Christ. Having understood the unity that exists in community, especially from her extensive study about the nature
of community, she understood profoundly the communion
that exists in the Mystical Body of Christ.[25] In community,
in which persons are united one with another, each member affects the others (as we will examine more closely in

[24] Edith Stein, "Love of the Cross: Some Thoughts for the Feast of St.
John of the Cross", in *The Collected Works of Edith Stein*, vol. 6, *The Hidden
Life: Hagiographic Essays, Meditations, Spiritual Texts*, trans. Waltraut Stein, ed.
L. Gelber and M. Linssen, O.C.D. (Washington, D.C.: ICS Publications,
1992), p. 92.

[25] See Edith Stein, "Individual and Community", in *The Collected Works of
Edith Stein*, vol. 7, *Philosophy of Psychology and the Humanities*, trans. Sister Mary
Catharine Baseheart, S.C.N., and Marianne Sawicki, ed. Marianne Sawicki
(Washington, D.C.: ICS Publications, 2000), pp. 129-314.

chapter 6); one member's sin or good deed affects the whole community. Venerable Pius XII explains: "As in the body when one member suffers, all the other members share its pain, and the healthy members come to the assistance of the ailing, so in the Church the individual members do not live for themselves alone, but also help their fellows, and all work in mutual collaboration for the common comfort and for the more perfect building up of the whole Body."[26]

In the community of mankind, the sin of Adam and Eve affected every member of the human family with the exception of the Blessed Virgin Mary. In the same way, Jesus, as God and as a member of the human family, died to atone for all of our sins. In a presentation she gave in 1930, before her entrance into Carmel, Edith wrote: "*Original Sin and Redemption* would remain wholly incomprehensible if humanity were the sum of wholly separate individuals and not a body with head and members (cf. Rom 12:5; 1 Cor 12:27). Only because in Adam *humanity as a nature* was created could his fall be the fall of all; only because Christ grows into this organism as an organ can the *grace of the head* overflow to all the members."[27]

Christ redeems us all, but He allows us to participate in His redemptive act, just as He allowed Simon of Cyrene to help

[26] Pius XII, Encyclical Letter *Mystici Corporis Christi* (Vatican City State: Libreria Editrice Vaticana, 1943), no. 15.

[27] Edith Stein, "Die theoretischen Grundlagen der sozialen Bildungsarbeit", in *Edith Stein Gesamtausgabe*, vol. 16, *Bildung und Entfaltung der Individualität: Beiträge zum christlichen Erziehungsauftrag*, ed. Sister Maria Amata Neyer, O.C.D., and Beate Beckmann-Zöller (Freiburg im Breisgau: Herder, 2001), p. 18. All translations from *Bildung und Entfaltung* by Sister M. Regina van den Berg, F.S.G.M.

Him to carry His Cross. When we are united with Christ our
Head, our sufferings can help to redeem souls. In this vein,
Sister Teresa Benedicta of the Cross, writing to her sisters in
Carmel in 1939, when the Second World War had already
broken out, explains:

> Do you hear the groans of the wounded on the battlefields
> in the west and the east? You are not a physician and not a
> nurse and cannot bind up the wounds. You are enclosed in
> a cell and cannot get to them. Do you hear the anguish of
> the dying? You would like to be a priest and comfort them.
> Does the lament of the widows and the orphans distress you?
> You would like to be an angel of mercy and help them. Look
> at the Crucified. If you are nuptially bound to him by the
> observance of your holy vows, your *being* is precious blood.
> Bound to him, you are omnipresent as he is. You cannot
> help here or there like the physician, the nurse, the priest.
> You can be at all fronts, wherever there is grief, in the power
> of the cross. Your compassionate love takes you everywhere,
> this love from the divine heart.[28]

[28] Stein, "Elevation of the Cross, September 14, 1939: *Ave Crux, Spes
Unica*", in *The Hidden Life*, p. 96. Cf. Pius XII, *Mystici Corporis Christi,* nos.
107–8: "As We write these words there passes before Our eyes, alas, an almost
endless throng of unfortunate beings for whom We shed tears of sorrow; sick,
poor, disabled, widows, orphans, and many not infrequently languishing even
unto death on account of their own painful trials or those of their families.
With the heart of a father We exhort all those who from whatever cause are
plunged in grief and anguish to lift their eyes trustfully to heaven and to offer
their sorrows to Him who will one day reward them abundantly. Let them all
remember that their sufferings are not in vain, but that they will turn to their
own immense gain and that of the Church, if to this end they bear them with
patience. The daily use of the offering made by the members of the Apostleship

How can we learn to embrace suffering? The answer that Edith Stein proposes, I think, is twofold. First, we must learn to have a wide vision, to live fully as members of the Mystical Body and to learn to see, by faith, that our actions and our sufferings affect others. Once she had embraced Catholicism, Edith immersed herself in the liturgical life of the Church, which, as she explains, helps us to widen our vision beyond our own needs and wants and to enter into the mystery of salvation.

Secondly, Edith Stein would, I think, help us to embrace suffering by counseling us to keep our eyes focused on the *effect* of our suffering. United to Christ, our suffering can save souls. All the small annoyances of life, all the inconveniences we endure, all the small unkindnesses we suffer from others— these can be united with Christ. For this reason, suffering well borne is not a cause for sadness, as Sister Teresa Benedicta explains in an essay she wrote for her sisters in Carmel:

---

of Prayer will contribute very much to make this intention more efficacious and We welcome this opportunity of recommending this Association highly, as one which is most pleasing to God.

"There never was a time, Venerable Brethren, when the salvation of souls did not impose on all the duty of associating their sufferings with the torments of our Divine Redeemer. But today that duty is more clear than ever, when a gigantic conflict has set almost the whole world on fire and leaves in its wake so much death, so much misery, so much hardship; in the same way today, in a special manner, it is the duty of all to fly from vice, the attraction of the world, the unrestrained pleasures of the body, and also from worldly frivolity and vanity which contribute nothing to the Christian training of the soul nor to the gaining of Heaven. Rather let those weighty words of Our immortal predecessor Leo the Great be deeply engraven upon our minds, that by Baptism we are made flesh of the Crucified: and that beautiful prayer of St. Ambrose: 'Carry me, Christ, on the Cross, which is salvation to the wanderers, sole rest for the wearied, wherein alone is life for those who die.'"

Thus, when someone desires to suffer, it is not merely a pious reminder of the suffering of the Lord. Voluntary expiatory suffering is what truly and really unites one to the Lord intimately.... Only someone whose spiritual eyes have been opened to the supernatural correlations of worldly events can desire suffering in expiation, and this is only possible for people in whom the spirit of Christ dwells, who as members [*Glieder*] are given life by the Head, receive his power, his meaning, and his direction. Conversely, works of expiation bind one closer to Christ, as every community that works together on one task becomes more closely knit as the limbs [*Glieder*] of a body, working together organically, continually become more strongly one.

But because *being* one with Christ is our sanctity, and progressively *becoming* one with him our happiness on earth, the love of the cross in no way contradicts being a joyful child of God. Helping Christ carry his cross fills one with a strong and pure joy, and those who may and can do so, the builders of God's kingdom, are the most authentic children of God.[29]

As a Christian, Edith Stein had learned to place her whole life in the hands of God and to receive all that life brought— both joys and sufferings—as coming from His hands. Already before her long-desired entrance into Carmel, Edith learned to be "led by God's hand and from God's hand, in the simplicity of the child and the humility of the Publican".[30]

---

[29] Stein, "Love of the Cross: Some Thoughts for the Feast of St. John of the Cross", in *The Hidden Life*, pp. 92–93.

[30] Edith Stein, "Das Weihnachtsgeheimnis: Menschwerdung und Menschheit", in *Ganzheitliches Leben*, p. 206.

Sister Teresa Benedicta understood that, as Christians, we can live fully in Christ, we can find our joy in Christ, only by participating in His suffering. Our communion with Christ is the most important and the most effective means of bringing communion to our entire world. When we are in communion with Christ, He will show us how we can further serve Him and how we can foster communion in our families, our Church, and our world.

2

Communion with Our Brothers and Sisters

The marvel of our being human is that we are not enclosed within ourselves, but are created so as to be able to transcend ourselves, to "go outside ourselves". We have "windows", so to speak, to the reality that exists outside of us. Our primary contact with reality is through our external senses, by means of which we see, hear, and touch the concrete things around us. Through our intellect we are able to come to know truths about the particular things we sense and are able to understand truths that surpass what we can know through our senses. Not all philosophers agree that we can know reality, but we will not engage them in the present context and will assume, with Edith Stein, the position of realism.

It was the realism of phenomenology that attracted Edith Stein and motivated her to study at Göttingen under Professor Edmund Husserl. During her years at Göttingen, the philosophers of the phenomenological school were fascinated by interpersonal realities, about how we can know what someone else is thinking, perceiving, judging, feeling, and it was therefore not surprising that Edith Stein devoted her doctoral dissertation to the phenomenon of empathy.

It is the ability of persons to know each other that makes communion between them possible. In his Apostolic Letter *Nuovo Millennio Ineunte*, Pope Saint John Paul II explains, as already noted, what communion with our brothers and sisters entails: "A spirituality of communion also means an ability to think of our brothers and sisters in faith within the profound unity of the Mystical Body, and therefore as 'those who are part of me.' This makes us able to share their joys and sufferings, to sense their desires and attend to their needs, to offer them deep and genuine friendship."[1] The spirituality of communion involves sharing the joys and the sufferings of our brothers and sisters, attending to their needs, and offering them deep and genuine friendship.

Sharing in another person's joy or sorrow means not only *understanding* the reason for his joy or sorrow, but, even more, it means *entering into* his joy or sorrow. Empathy is this *entering into* another person's feeling. In addition to knowing about other persons, we can also, maintains Edith Stein, enter, in some way, into their subjectivity. We can actually *in-feel* another person's feelings, and when we do, we experience him "from within". Such a sharing in his joys and sorrows from within helps us to establish communion with him.

At the outset, it is important to clarify that the human person is not *wholly* open to others. Edith Stein emphasizes that a certain level of the human person—the level she calls the soul—is in principle inaccessible to other human persons.

---

[1] John Paul II, Apostolic Letter *Novo Millennio Ineunte* (Boston: Pauline Books and Media, 2001), no. 43.

Each person has a hidden depth, known only to God, who created the soul.

The Nature of Empathy

When she begins to explain something, Edith Stein's typical method is to offer an example. She employs this method when explaining empathy: "A friend tells me that he has lost his brother and I become aware of his pain."[2] The awareness of the pain is distinct from outer perception. In perception, the senses provide data: they give the pale and disturbed face, the toneless and strained voice of the grieving friend, but they do not give his pain. Empathy gives the pain, not the pale face and the strained voice. This pain is perceived simultaneously *with* the features received through outer perception. In virtue of empathy, we have a direct awareness of another's experience, and it is this experience that Edith Stein wants to examine more closely.

Einfühlung, the German word for "empathy", literally means "in-feeling". In empathy I transcend myself, in a certain sense, and spiritually and mentally enter into the experience of the other person to turn with him to his object. When empathy first arises, the other's psychic state "faces me as an object".[3] When I try to understand the other's psychic

[2] *The Collected Works of Edith Stein*, vol. 3, *On the Problem of Empathy*, 3rd ed., trans. Waltraut Stein (Washington, D.C.: ICS Publications, 1989), p. 6.
[3] Ibid., p. 10.

state more clearly, I allow myself to be drawn into the content of his experience (his sorrow, in this case), so that his sorrow is no longer an object, because "the content, having pulled me into it, is no longer really an object".[4] The fullness of empathy is this "submerging ourselves in the foreign experience",[5] in which "I am at the foreign 'I' and explain its experience by living it after the other."[6] It is not the case that the feeling I experience empathically becomes my own; it retains the character of belonging to the other.

Empathic joy is different from our own joy. Higher-level feelings, which Edith Stein calls "spiritual feelings", are directed toward and motivated by an object; they are intentional.[7] My joy is motivated, for example, by good news that I received. The empathic joy does not come from myself but from another. I experience joy, but the joy is not mine. When I experience joy directly, I experience it as arising from within me. In empathic joy, I experience the joy as coming from someone else. Still, in both cases I truly experience joy.

[4] Ibid.
[5] Ibid., p. 23.
[6] Ibid., p. 34.
[7] Edith Stein distinguishes three types of feelings. The first and lowest level are purely physical sensations, such as feelings of warmth or pain. Psychic feelings include pleasure in feeling warmth, general feelings, and moods. The first two levels of feelings simply overcome us and arise without our consent. Often we do not even know where these feelings come from. In addition, not all of these feelings are intentional (i.e., directed toward an object). The highest level of feelings are characterized by being intentional; they are always directed *toward* something, and the person knows the reason for his feeling (which is not always the case in psychic feelings, such as moods). I can be joyful *because* I have been forgiven or be filled with sorrow *because* a loved one has died, for example.

When I empathically feel the sorrow another feels at the death of a loved one, I genuinely share in the other's sorrow because I am able to in-feel it. I am able to empathize with the other by knowing the motive of his feelings and by "reading" the sorrow in his grieved face, his strained voice, et cetera. The empathized content is not shared in *all* its peculiarity, because only its essential meaning is empathically available. No one can experience *exactly* my joy or sorrow, but through empathy another can experience the *sense* (meaning) of the feeling.

It is possible, through empathy, to experience empathically what I have never experienced primordially.[8] Although I have never grieved for the loss of my brother, I can empathically experience this loss through another. Empathy enables us to enlarge our experience to include many things we would not experience if we were enclosed within ourselves and limited to our own direct experience. It is not uncommon to hear it said, "I cannot understand your situation because I have never been in it myself." Such a notion indicates a misunderstanding of empathy, because through empathy we are able to do precisely that: to enter into another's experience.

The phenomenon of empathy can be brought to greater clarity by distinguishing it from related phenomena. Empathy is not a process of inference. We do not infer from the observable to the unobservable. A mother does not treat her

---

[8] See Stein, *On the Problem of Empathy*, p. 115: "I can experience values empathically and discover correlative levels of my person, even though my primordial experience has not yet presented an opportunity for their exposure. He who has never looked a danger in the face himself can still experience himself as brave or cowardly in the empathic representation of another's situation."

infant's cry as evidence to be used as the basis for an inference that allows her to arrive at the conclusion that the infant is in need. Rather, the mother knows directly *in* the scream that the infant is in need. We would consider it very strange if someone treated a tear-stained face as evidence that he uses to arrive at a conclusion.

Empathy is not putting ourselves in the place of the other (that is, imagining ourselves in his shoes, so to speak). In such a case, once we have the appropriate experience, we again "concede to the foreign 'I' its place and ascribe this experience to him".[9] We, as it were, picture ourselves in his situation and then ascribe the experience that *we* would have to *him*. This, Edith Stein says, is a "surrogate for empathy" that one may call an "assumption", but not empathy itself.[10]

Neither is empathy what philosophers call fellow-feeling (*Mitfühlen*), in which a feeling is *shared* between two individuals. The same event can be joyful for another as well as for me so that we share the *same* joy. Parents who rejoice over the birth of their child have fellow-feeling; they experience the joy in common. Unlike fellow-feeling, the feeling in empathy is nonprimordial; that is, it does not originate in *me* but in the other. Even in fellow-feeling, however, empathy is the manner in which we learn that another shares our feeling.

The experience of empathy does not eliminate the experience of there being two persons. Empathy is therefore also distinct from a feeling of oneness (*Einsfühlung*). There is,

[9] Ibid., p. 14.
[10] Ibid.

Edith Stein concedes, such a thing as an experience of one-ness, but it is not the same as empathy.[11]

Lastly, empathy is not the same as taking the other's feeling upon oneself, as happens in the case of contagion (*Gefühl-sansteckung*). In the case of contagion, I may, finding myself in a cheerful atmosphere, be "swept up" by the prevailing joy and become cheerful myself. When I take another's feeling upon myself in contagion, I am not directed *toward* the other's feeling as I am in empathy; in fact, I need not even recognize that the other is feeling cheerful. Contagion does not announce the other's experience, as empathy does. It may be the case that I realize only afterward that my cheerful mood is the effect of having been among a cheerful group of people. No empathy can take place without recognizing the other's state.[12]

Developing Empathy

Empathy is a type of perception, even if it is distinct from sensual perception.[13] Just as we do not *will* to see or to hear, so, in the same way, we cannot *will* to empathize. We can, however, do certain things to enhance our ability to empathize with others, and we can also remove obstacles that prevent us from empathizing with others. Moreover, there are certain personal qualities that can either hinder or enhance empathy.

[11] See ibid., pp. 16ff.
[12] See ibid., pp. 23, 31, 71ff.
[13] See ibid., p. 11.

Sometimes we fail to empathize because of a lack of attention to another. We can fail to notice the joy or sorrow in someone else when we are wholly preoccupied with some other affair. The example that Edith Stein uses is the following: "I am completely filled with grief over a bereavement at the moment my friend tells me the joyful news."[14] The grief may be so strong that I simply *cannot* empathize with my friend's joy.

It is also possible, although Edith Stein does not mention it, that we cannot empathize because we are selfishly engrossed in our own affairs, or because some vice makes us interested only in ourselves. If we are overly concerned about ourselves, to the exclusion of others, then we are, as it were, locked within ourselves and cannot empathize. At the end of his *Christian Ethics*, Dietrich von Hildebrand[15] shows that certain vices, such as lust or pride, blind us to the good. Those who are slaves to concupiscence approach every situation "by the question of how much pleasure they get out of it".[16] They choose to close themselves to the good because

[14] Ibid., p. 15.

[15] Born October 12, 1889, in Florence, Italy, of German parents, Dietrich von Hildebrand studied philosophy under Edmund Husserl, although he had already completed his studies in Göttingen by the time Edith Stein arrived. In 1938, he and his wife fled Germany and eventually settled in the United States in 1940. He taught for many years at Fordham University in New York City and died in 1977. Edith Stein and Dietrich von Hildebrand knew one another, and they had a few brief encounters. See Alice von Hildebrand, *Dietrich von Hildebrand and Edith Stein: Husserl's Students* (Fort Collins, Col.: Roman Catholic Books, 2013), pp. 34ff.

[16] Dietrich von Hildebrand, *Christian Ethics* (New York: David McKay Company, 1953), p. 431.

"the concupiscent attitude as such necessarily implies that indifference toward the important-in-itself."[17] Like the concupiscent person, the proud person is wholly self-centered and is thereby blinded to any values transcendent to his own. I would add that these vices also thwart empathy inasmuch as they blind one to others in the same way they blind one to objective good.

While some vices hinder empathy, virtues would seem to open one to empathy. The virtue of charity, for example, naturally enhances empathy (perhaps the converse is also true: empathy enhances charity). When we love someone, we are constantly interested in him and naturally desire to empathize with him more deeply. How else would we discover how to please him but through empathy? It is easy, it seems, to share the joys and sufferings of those we love; in fact, it is quite natural to do so. It is not as easy to share the joys and sufferings of those we hardly know and even less easy to share those of mankind in general.

Empathy presupposes, moreover, an openness to and an interest in the other as a *person* who has experiences of joy and sorrow. We must be *willing* and *interested* to enter into another person's experience. Pope Saint John Paul II had such an interest in others as persons. In his Apostolic Letter *Novo Millennio Ineunte* he makes an observation that reveals this interest: "I have been impressed this year by the crowds of people which have filled St. Peter's Square at the many celebrations. I have often stopped to look at the long queues

[17] Ibid., 432.

of pilgrims waiting patiently to go through the Holy Door. In each of them I tried to imagine the story of a life, made of up joys, worries, sufferings; the story of someone whom Christ has met and who, in dialogue with him, was setting out again on a journey of hope."[18] Rather than seeing a crowd, Pope Saint John Paul II saw each person as an individual with his own joys and sorrows.

Empathy is important, then, in our consideration of how to foster a spirituality of communion. Once we understand a brother or a sister from within, we can serve, guide, and comfort in a way that is not possible without empathy. We all have experienced the difference between attention that arises through empathy and that which does not. With empathy comes the personal touch, the attention to what I as an individual feel and experience. Without empathy, the kind word, the helping hand, the comfort given all seem impersonal and cold, somehow misplaced. Unless we empathize, we do not know exactly how to help, to comfort, to love.[19]

Edith Stein not only wrote about empathy but also had a natural facility for empathizing with others. Being selfless and generous helped her to in-feel others. One of her sisters in Carmel relates: "At a certain point in the novitiate, when I was feeling depressed, it was Edith Stein who, as inconspicuously as possible, did everything she could to cheer me up. She found all kinds of opportunities for doing me favors or whispering a word of encouragement. She had a genius

---

[18] John Paul II, *Novo Millennio Ineunte*, no. 8.
[19] Empathy is thus related to the virtue of prudence.

for coming up with exactly the right thing."[20] The same sister also recounts: "On one evening when I was feeling very depressed, Edith Stein was in the pantry putting away the dishes. The great silence had already begun. I think she must have sensed my mood, because, even though she couldn't talk to me, she came over and gave me a beautiful, friendly smile. That's something I'll never forget. It made my troubles instantly vanish."[21]

Empathy is essential for those people who guide or counsel others. Absent empathy, we are necessarily limited by our own experience, and we can counsel only to the extent that our experiences will allow. Of course, our ability to guide and counsel increases as our own experience increases; however, through empathy we can truly enter into the difficulties another person faces, understand how he experiences the situation, and know how to guide him, based not only on the objective situation, but also on how the individual is experiencing it.

Empathy in the Spiritual Life

Empathy is important not only in establishing communion with our brothers and sisters, but also in attaining union with Christ. Rolf Kühn, writing about Edith Stein's notion of empathy, comments that empathy is so applicable to the

[20] Sister Electa (Cologne Carmel, Edith Stein Archives), in Waltraud Herbstrith, *Edith Stein: A Biography*, 2nd ed., trans. Father Bernard Bonowitz, O.C.S.O. (San Francisco: Ignatius Press, 1992), p. 127.
[21] Ibid., p. 137.

life of prayer that one could say that "the mystical life is the proper practice of empathy."[22]

Empathy in prayer is not the same as realizing another person is sad by looking at his face and hearing his voice. How, after all, can we in-feel God when He is physically absent? Edith explains that whenever there is empathy, "the object itself is present here and now."[23] God is not physically present. It is true that, in our everyday experience, we can sometimes empathize with someone who is physically absent. A friend can write or call to relate the loss of his brother, and I can become aware of his pain. Certainly, it is *easier* for me to empathize when the friend is physically present and I can see his face and hear his voice, but it is possible to empathize to a certain extent when the friend is not physically present.[24]

In *Novo Millennio Ineunte*, Pope Saint John Paul II exhorts us to contemplate the face of Jesus, so that we may make His face shine before the world.[25] We cannot physically see the face of Jesus and therefore cannot in-feel His sentiments by reading His face. We attain the vision of His face, John Paul II explains, through faith. The face of Christ emerges in the Gospels. Even for the apostles, who physically saw the

[22] Rolf Kühn, "Leben aus dem Sein: Zur philosopischen Grundintuitionen Edith Steins", in *Freiburger Zeitschrift für Philosophie und Theologie* 35 (1988): p. 16. Translation by Sister M. Regina van den Berg, F.S.G.M.

[23] Stein, *On the Problem of Empathy*, p. 7.

[24] In this context, it would be interesting to examine the effect of modern communications technology on interpersonal relationships and the development of empathy.

[25] See John Paul II, *Novo Millennio Ineunte*, chap. 2.

face of Christ, "*only faith could fully enter the mystery of that face.*"[26] Faith alone, says Sister Teresa Benedicta of the Cross, "gives knowledge of God. And how is one to arrive at union with God without knowing him?"[27] In this life, when God is not visibly present, we know Him through Sacred Scripture, the Sacred Liturgy, and the Magisterium of the Church. The Christian who desires empathic union with God will return again and again to these sources that make God present for us.

Empathy is not isolated from our knowledge *about* a person; in fact, knowing more about another can prevent and correct mistakes in empathy. If I know that a person cries for joy, I will not make the mistake of empathically assuming tears to betoken sadness. In the same way, our knowledge of God helps us to empathize with Him. Edith Stein emphasized the importance of such knowledge. Speaking of the responsibility of teachers for the formation of youth, she writes:

> Thorough dogmatic formation is essential; that is, one must have the truths of the Faith not only ready in memory, but one must grasp them in their organic connection and in their meaning. These truths must be the inner form of one's spirit; that is, they must be so much a part of oneself that one can

---

[26] Ibid., no. 19.

[27] *The Collected Works of Edith Stein*, vol. 6, *The Science of the Cross*, trans. Sister Josephine Koeppel, O.C.D., ed. L. Gelber and R. Leuven, O.C.D. (Washington, D.C.: ICS Publications, 2002), p. 59. The knowledge of faith, Sister Teresa Benedicta adds, is a distinct kind of knowledge. In comparison with natural knowledge, "faith is a totally dark night for the soul. But it is precisely by these means that it brings her light: a knowledge of perfect certainty that exceeds all other knowledge and science so that one can arrive in perfect contemplation at a correct conception of faith" (ibid., p. 58).

at any time apply them to the demands of the moment. One gains such a dogmatic knowledge only, of course, through continual study of the teachings of the Faith: through the definitions of the dogmas themselves, the works of the Fathers of the Church and other learned teachers, with classical and modern theological works.[28]

Through empathy with Christ attained through faith and through knowledge of Him, I can unite myself with His Cross and suffer *with* Him in His sorrow. It is not the case that I join my sufferings to His, but that I empathize with *His* sufferings. Saint Paul says that he wishes only "that I may know him ... and may share his sufferings, becoming like him in his death".[29]

Many of our Catholic devotional practices can assist us in achieving this empathic union with Christ. The Stations of the Cross and the mysteries of the Rosary permit us to enter into the circumstances of Christ's life in order to empathize with Him. Devotion to the Sacred Heart teaches us that Christ has a heart, an affective life, and our devotion to His Heart is meant to inspire us to in-feel what Christ feels, so that we may love what He loves and do what pleases Him. Edith Stein remarks that "complete consecration to the Divine Heart is reached only when He is our home, our daily residence, and the center of our lives—when His life has become our

---

[28] Edith Stein, "Die Mitwirkung der klösterlichen Bildungsanstalten an der religiösen Bildung der Jugend", in *Edith Stein Gesamtausgabe*, vol. 16, *Bildung und Entfaltung der Individualität: Beiträge zum christlichen Erziehungsauftrag*, ed. Sister Maria Amata Neyer, O.C.D., and Beate Beckmann-Zöller (Freiburg im Breisgau: Herder, 2001), p. 56.

[29] Phil 3:10.

life."[30] Christ's pierced Heart also teaches us that His Heart is *open* for our in-feeling; He permits us to empathize with Him. Edith Stein writes, "Jesus allowed His side to be opened ... to show us that He opens His Heart for us. It is presented to us as a place for us to reside. Our soul can enter Jesus' soul because both are spiritual. Just so, Jesus comes into our heart; that is, He comes into our most inner being in Holy Communion. Our turning to Him is spiritual communion."[31]

The eucharistic life, explains Edith Stein, is the most fruitful place to learn to empathize with Christ because, through the Eucharist, Christ permits us to share His life. She explains that, in the Eucharist,

> He also permits us to *share His life*, especially when we participate in the *Liturgy*, and thereby experience with Him His life, His suffering and death, His Resurrection and Ascension, the birth and growth of His Church. Then we are lifted above the confinement of our own being into the expanse of the Kingdom of God. His concerns become ours; we become ever more deeply united with the Lord and live with Him with all our being. All loneliness ceases, and we are wholly secure in the King's tent; we walk in His light.[32]

[30] Stein, "Eucharistische Erziehung", in *Bildung und Entfaltung der Individualität*, p. 66.

[31] Edith Stein, "Das Herz Jesu—Unsere Wohnung" (Cologne Carmel: Edith Stein Archives), in Antony Kavunguvalappil, O.C.D., *Theology of Suffering and the Cross in the Life and Works of Blessed Edith Stein*, European University Studies, vol. 642 (Frankfurt am Main: Peter Lang, 1998), p. 183. Translated by Sister M. Regina van den Berg, F.S.G.M.

[32] Stein, "Eucharistische Erziehung", in *Bildung und Entfaltung der Individualität*, p. 65.

In empathizing with Christ, we are elevated beyond ourselves. Having in-felt Christ's motives and desires, we are
called to make these motives and desires our own: to put on
the mind of Christ.[33] Sharing Christ's longing for the salvation of all, we will, like Christ, be willing to suffer for
the sake of souls, knowing that, in virtue of being united
in the community of the Mystical Body, one member can
help another. Having been inflamed with a Christ-like love
for souls, we will desire communion with our brothers and
sisters. Through empathy, we are able to know others, even
when their experiences are vastly different from ours. By
means of empathy, too, we can more effectively love, serve,
counsel, and comfort our brothers and sisters.

[33] Cf. Phil 2:5.

3

Communion between Man and Woman

As a young adult in the early 1900s, Edith Stein was an active
feminist. A university education had only recently become
available for women, and Edith was among the first women
to avail herself of the new opportunity. She was an avid
advocate for a woman's right to vote and wanted to devote
herself to a career.[1] Once she obtained her doctorate in philosophy, Edith realized that not all careers were as yet open to
women, since she was unable—despite her talent—to obtain
a teaching position at the university.[2] After her conversion

[1] See *The Collected Works of Edith Stein*, vol. 1, *Life in a Jewish Family (1891–
1916)*, trans. Sister Josephine Koeppel, O.C.D., ed. L. Gelber and R. Leuven,
O.C.D. (Washington, D.C.: ICS Publications, 1986), p. 123: "We often dis-
cussed the issue of a double career. Erna and our two girl friends had many
misgivings, wondering whether one ought not give up a career for the sake
of marriage. I was alone in maintaining, always, that I would not sacrifice my
profession on any account."

[2] See Stein to Fritz Kaufmann, November 8, 1919, in *The Collected Works
of Edith Stein*, vol. 5, *Edith Stein: Self-Portrait in Letters*, trans. Sister Josephine
Koeppel, O.C.D., ed. L. Gelber and R. Leuven, O.C.D. (Washington, D.C.:
ICS Publications, 1993), no. 31, p. 35: "A *pre-commission* had decided not
even to judge my thesis since the habilitation of women continues to create many difficulties." Cf. Letter of Professor Dr. Edmund Husserl, in *Kölner Selig- und Heiligsprechungsprozess der Dienerin Gottes Sr. Teresia Benedicta*

to Catholicism, she gave up the idea of teaching at the university, thinking, at first, that a career and research were not compatible with her newfound faith. She writes: "Immediately before, and for a good while after my conversion, I was of the opinion that to lead a religious life meant one had to give up all that was secular and to live totally immersed in thoughts of the Divine."[3] Edith then no longer concerned herself with women's rights, and she said that she had no more interest in the matter.[4] After teaching at the Dominican teachers' training college for several years, she began, in 1927, to offer lectures throughout Germany and abroad upon request. Realizing that the relationship between man and woman was an important topic at the time, she began to give lectures on the nature and vocation of woman.[5]

Edith Stein holds that since God created man *and* woman, there must be a distinct role for each. When we attempt to

---

a Cruce (Edith Stein): Professe und Chorschwester des Ordens der Allerseligsten Jungfrau Maria vom Berge Karmel (Cologne: Kloster der Karmelitinnen "Maria vom Frieden", 1962), p. 5, no. 7: "Miss Dr. Stein has acquired a wide and in-depth education of philosophy, and her ability for independent and scientific research and teaching are without question. If the academic professions were to be opened to women, I would most highly recommend her, above others, for admission to the profession."

[3] Stein to Sister Callista Kopf, O.P., February 12, 1928, in Stein, *Self-Portrait in Letters*, no. 45, p. 54.

[4] See Stein to Sister Callista Kopf, O.P., August 18, 1931, in ibid., no. 100, p. 99: "During my years in the *Gymnasium* and as a young student [at the university], I was a radical feminist. Then I lost interest in the whole question. Now, because I am obliged to do so, I seek purely objective solutions."

[5] Some of these writings are in *The Collected Works of Edith Stein*, vol. 2, *Essays on Woman*, trans. Freda Mary Oben, ed. L. Gelber and R. Leuven, O.C.D., 2nd rev. ed. (Washington, D.C.: ICS Publications, 1996).

deny or to change the role we are created to have, conflict and strife arise, both within our very being and in our relationships with others. If God has created men and women to be different, not only physically, but also spiritually, emotionally, and intellectually, and if He has a particular role in mind for each of the sexes, then we can live the spirit of communion only by living in accord with our nature.

Differences between Man and Woman

Edith Stein's essay "The Separate Vocations of Man and Woman according to Nature and Grace"[6] takes an approach similar to that of Pope John Paul II in his Wednesday General Audiences that were collected under the title *The Original Unity of Man and Woman: Catechesis on the Book of Genesis*. Both begin their discussion of sexual differences with the biblical story of the creation.

The differences between man and woman are proclaimed in the first pages of Sacred Scripture. Genesis recounts that God made man "in His image", making them male and female. Although separated into the sexes, human persons have a common vocation. God commands them both: "Be fruitful and multiply, and fill the earth and subdue it; and have dominion over the fish of the sea and over the birds of the air and over every living thing that moves upon the earth."[7]

---

[6]Stein, "The Separate Vocations of Man and Woman according to Nature and Grace", in ibid., chap. 2, pp. 59ff.

[7]Gen 1:28.

The task of responsibility for the earth belongs to *both* man and woman. They have equality and shared responsibility.

Saint John Paul II explains that the creation of Eve from Adam's rib emphasizes the equality between the sexes. Man and woman share the same humanity.[8] Adam recognizes this when upon waking from his sleep and seeing Eve for the first time he exclaims, "This at last is bone of my bones and flesh of my flesh; she shall be called Woman, because she was taken out of Man."[9] Man and woman are to be companions; they are meant to live together in harmony and complementarity. Adam and Eve were called to live in an intimate communion: "We are to consider the life of the initial human pair as the most intimate community of love, that their faculties were in perfect harmony as within one single being."[10] While Edith Stein continues to speak primarily of the differences between man and woman, it is important to remember, too, that there is a basic unity between them.

Sacred Scripture recounts the first conflict between Adam and Eve after the Fall. When God questions Adam about his deed, he blames the woman: "The woman whom you gave to be with me, she gave me fruit of the tree, and I ate."[11] No longer are Adam and Eve of one heart and mind.

It is interesting, as Edith Stein notes, that Adam and Eve receive different punishments after the Fall. Adam's

[8] See John Paul II, *The Original Unity of Man and Woman* (Boston: Daughters of St. Paul, 1981), pp. 65ff.

[9] Gen 2:23.

[10] Stein, "The Separate Vocations of Man and Woman according to Nature and Grace", in *Essays on Woman*, p. 62.

[11] Gen 3:12.

punishment concerns his work: "Cursed is the ground because of you; in toil you shall eat of it all the days of your life."[12] Eve is told: "I will greatly multiply your pain in childbearing; in pain you shall bring forth children, yet your desire shall be for your husband, and he shall rule over you."[13] The distinct punishments point to the distinct roles of man and woman.

Edith Stein affirms that man's "body and soul are equipped to fight and conquer [the world] ..., to *understand* it and by knowledge to make it his own, to *possess* and *enjoy* it, and, finally, to make it in a sense his own *creation* through *purposeful activity*."[14] Man's greater physical strength enables him to protect and to fight. Adam's punishment concerns his work, and men, says Edith Stein, are spiritually equipped for their work by a more *objective* approach to life. Men, more easily than women, can be detached from their emotions and feelings in order to view concerns objectively.

The woman is physically created to bear and to nurse children: "The primary calling of woman is the procreation and raising of children."[15] The differences between men and women are not *solely* physical, reasons Edith Stein. If God made woman *physically* able to bear and to nurse children, then He must also have equipped her *spiritually* for this task. Moreover, given that the soul is the form of the body, Stein

---

[12] Gen 3:17.

[13] Gen 3:16.

[14] Stein, "The Separate Vocations of Man and Woman according to Nature and Grace", in *Essays on Woman*, pp. 70–71.

[15] Stein, "Spirituality of the Christian Woman", in *Essays on Woman*, p. 100.

suggests that the souls of man and woman must somehow be distinct.[16]

Unlike man, woman is decidedly *subjective*. By this term Stein means that abstract thought and objects usually do not interest woman as much as persons do. Edith Stein writes: "Woman naturally seeks to embrace that which is *living, personal, and whole*. To cherish, guard, protect, nourish and advance growth is her natural, maternal yearning. Lifeless matter, the *fact*, can hold primary interest for her only insofar as it serves the living and personal, not ordinarily for its own sake. Relevant to this is another matter: *abstraction in every sense* is alien to the feminine nature."[17]

In her work, woman is motivated primarily by *persons*. Whereas a man is more likely to enjoy work for its own sake, a woman will enjoy her work because she is serving another in some way. For this reason, she finds it easier to share in another's life, to take part in all that concerns another. Rather than being the one who holds primary responsibility, she often finds her joy in serving others.

Whereas intellect predominates in the life of man, Edith Stein maintains that feelings and emotions are particularly strong influences in the life of woman: "The strength of woman lies in the emotional life.... The emotions, the

[16]Cf. Stein to Sister Callista Kopf, O.P., August 18, 1931, in Stein, *Self-Portrait in Letters*, no. 100, p. 99: "The insistence that sexual differences are 'stipulated by the body alone' is questionable from various points of view. 1) If *anima = forma corporis*, then bodily differentiation constitutes an index of differentiation in the spirit. 2) Matter serves form, not the reverse. That strongly suggests that the difference in the psyche is the primary one."

[17]Stein, "The Ethos of Women's Professions", in *Essays on Woman*, p. 45.

essential organ for comprehension of the existent in its total-
ity and in its peculiarity, occupy the center of her being."[18]
Empathy, therefore, is a particularly feminine quality. Edith
Stein notes that the strong emphasis on emotions allows
mothers to have a keen sense of their children's needs and
the sensitivity to know how best to guide them.[19] The natural attitude of women toward the whole and the personal fits
her for her roles as mother and spouse.

Every woman, Edith Stein maintains, is created to be both
mother and spouse in some sense, just as every man is called
to be a father and spouse in some sense. Not every woman
is called by God to the married life; therefore, not every
woman will be a biological mother. The consecrated woman
and the single woman are also called to be mothers. In their
maternal way, they are to nurture and to guard the natural
and supernatural lives of those in their care.

The differences between man and woman affect their relationship with Christ. In his following of Christ, a man may
more easily be motivated by the *mission* of Christ. A woman's spirituality is motivated, rather, by the *Person* of Christ
and by her relationship with Him. The image of the consecrated woman as the bride of Christ emphasizes this aspect.
Of course, both men and women need to have a relationship with the Person of Christ and need to share in His mission. As a matter of emphasis and natural tendency, though,
men seem to identify more naturally with Christ's mission,
and women with the person of Christ.

---

[18] Stein, "Spirituality of the Christian Woman", in *Essays on Woman*, p. 96.
[19] See ibid., p. 109.

Generalizations about Men and Women

Clearly, the generalizations that Edith Stein makes about the nature of man and woman do not apply in every case, but they are true enough in general to be worthy of our consideration. She herself says that some "women may closely approximate the masculine type" and continues to explain: "If on the whole, marriage and motherhood are the primary vocations for the feminine sex, it is not necessarily true for each individual. Women may be called to singular cultural achievements, and their talents may be adapted to these achievements."[20]

When we compare what we know of Edith Stein with her account of the nature of woman, she may at first appear not to fit her own description well at all.[21] Already as a young child, she was interested in studies for their own sake, it seems. Although her classmates describe her as a kind person and a

[20] Stein, "Problems of Women's Education", in *Essays on Woman*, p. 189.

[21] Cf. Hilda C. Graef, *The Scholar and the Cross: The Life and Work of Edith Stein* (Maryland: The Newman Press, 1955), p. 76: "Perhaps it might be objected that in thus describing the nature of woman she actually excludes herself. Is she herself not really interested in things for their own sake, is she not a philosopher coolly analyzing 'phenomena,' living in a world of abstractions? This would be a very erroneous conception. All her male friends, a Father Przywara and an Abbot Walzer, stress her tender femininity; and though she had a philosophical mind, she had a typically feminine one in that she did not philosophize by deduction from principles. The phenomenological way is in fact singularly adapted to a feminine mind, since it is concerned with 'phenomena' as they surround and affect us, regarding everything as much as possible as a whole, finding what it really is by the intuitive glance of a mind that loves and reverences reality as it is. Such philosophizing is not foreign to the feminine mind as she describes it, though of course the gift of any form of philosophical mind is rarer in women even than it is in men."

good friend, it was obvious to everyone that learning was her
real passion. At the university she did not study a practical or
person-oriented discipline (her uncle tried to persuade her to
study medicine, but she declined) but chose one of the most
abstract of fields—philosophy.[22] Her conversion, moreover,
was occasioned, at least in large part, by reading the autobiography of Saint Teresa of Jesus, which led her to study the
catechism and the missal and seek baptism. At the process for
her beatification and canonization, it was attested that "her
conversion did not occur as a result of her being emotionally
moved, but it occurred on the path of intellectual insight."[23]
As will be further illustrated in chapter 4, her life was marked
by an iron will; she seemed to have her emotions and her
desires wholly under control.

All these characteristics, and more could be added, seem to
fit Edith Stein's description of the masculine nature insofar as
they point to an objectivity, an emphasis on the factual and
intellectual, and a dominance of the will over the emotions.
Saint Teresa of Jesus, who encouraged her daughters to be like
strong men, would have delighted to know that one of her
Carmelite daughters would possess these features so strongly.[24]

[22] See Stein, *Life in a Jewish Family*, p. 64.

[23] *Kölner Selig- und Heiligsprechungsprozess der Dienerin Gottes Sr. Teresia Benedicta a Cruce (Edith Stein): Professe und Chorschwester des Ordens der Allerseligsten
Jungfrau Maria vom Berge Karmel*, p. 25, no. 30.

[24] See Teresa of Ávila, *The Way of Perfection*, trans. and ed. E. Allison Peers
(New York: Image Books, 2004), p. 130: "Therefore, sisters, have no fear that
you will die of thirst on this road; you will never lack so much of the water of
comfort that your thirst will be intolerable; so take my advice and do not tarry
on the way, but strive like strong men until you die in the attempt, for you are
here for nothing else than to strive."

For all that, these undeniably masculine characteristics in Edith Stein are embodied in a particularly feminine manner.

Even in her intellectual and objective quest for truth, the feminine emphasis on the person was present. Her doctoral dissertation was about empathy, the ability to in-feel other persons. Roman Ingarden, who gave Edith Stein helpful comments on the work of her dissertation, writes: "What interested her most was the question of defining the possibility of mutual communication between human beings, the possibility of establishing community. This was more than a theoretical concern for her; belonging to a community was a personal necessity, something that vitally affected her identity."[25]

Although Edith Stein's conversion was occasioned in large part by her reading of a book, this reading was more akin to meeting a person than to learning new facts, for the book was the story of the saint's life, not an exposition of the truths of the Faith. More than likely, it was the appeal of the person of Saint Teresa of Jesus that so captivated Edith that she stayed up all night reading the book.

Overcoming Typical Faults

Since the Fall, both men and women have typical faults and tendencies to sin. In his fallen nature, Edith Stein explains, a man tends to become one-sided. He may wholly lose himself

---

[25] Roman Ingarden, *Über die philosophischen Forschungen Edith Steins*, p. 473, in Waltraud Herbstrith, *Edith Stein: A Biography*, trans. Father Bernard Bonowitz, O.C.S.O., 2nd ed. (San Francisco: Ignatius Press, 1992), p. 146.

in his work, for example, and lose interest in his family. With the greater tendency to be interested in *things* for their own sake, a man can easily become "consumed" by his enterprise and expect others to share his interest.

Man also tends to strive for perfection in a given area, without respecting the human limitations imposed upon him. In wanting to know, for instance, he is tempted to seek to explain all things in human fashion. Seeking to conquer in the area of knowledge, he may fail to respect the limits set upon knowledge or the moral limits set upon scientific research. The contemporary attempt to clone man can be offered as an example of such one-sidedness. Those who seek to clone human beings ignore the moral limitations of the natural moral law, because, we may suppose, they are driven by the desire to accomplish the feat. In their one-sided striving for the goal, they neglect other more important aspects. Failing to recognize God as Creator, man places himself and his endeavors first. In this one-sidedness, men tend to use other human beings for their own ends and projects.

Women typically fail in the opposite way: whereas men tend to lack the personal attitude, women fail by being too focused on persons and losing sight of objective facts. Edith Stein colorfully describes typical feminine faults:

> Usually, the *personal outlook* appears to be exaggerated unwholesomely; in the first place, her inclination to center both her activities and those of others about her own person is expressed by vanity, desire for praise and recognition, and an unchecked need for communication; on the other hand,

it is seen in an excessive interest in others as in curiosity, gossip, and an indiscreet need to penetrate into the intimate life of others. *Her view reaching toward the whole* leads easily to a frittering away of her powers: her antipathy for the necessary objective disciplining of individual abilities results in her superficial nibbling in all areas. And in her relation to others, it is manifested in her complete absorption with them beyond the measure required by the maternal functions: the sympathetic mate becomes the obtrusive mischief-maker who cannot endure quiet, reserved growth; and because of this, she does not foster development but rather hinders and paralyzes it.[26]

Unfortunately, contemporary society actually *promotes* and *encourages* these typical feminine faults and sins, and this makes it more difficult for women to avoid or to overcome them. Advertisements and television shows encourage women to live on a sensual level and to care excessively for their bodily appearance. Women are, moreover, encouraged to be curious about things that do not concern them and to engage in destructive gossip. The number of magazines that promote such curiosity and gossip at the checkout lines of grocery stores is disheartening. To avoid the typical feminine faults in contemporary society is a formidable challenge. Control of the senses and ascetical practices must be essential components in our efforts to overcome or avoid these faults.

How can women protect themselves against typical feminine sins, faults, and weaknesses? First of all, Edith Stein

[26] Stein, "The Ethos of Women's Professions", in *Essays on Woman*, p. 47.

mentions objective work as a good remedy and preventive:
"A good natural remedy against all typical feminine defects is
solid objective work. This demands in itself the repression of
an excessively personal attitude. It calls for an end to superfi-
ciality not only in her own work but in general."[27] For this
reason, Edith Stein thinks that, although a married woman's
primary responsibility is her family, it may sometimes be good
for her to work outside the home, because this protects her
from becoming curiously and intrusively involved in other
people's lives, as well as from becoming selfishly concerned
only with herself.

Because in a woman there seems to be a closer union
between soul and body, it is easier and more dangerous for her
to become overly sensual. If she gives the body more than it
needs, physical nature begins to demand more, and it does so
to the detriment of her spiritual good: "Instead of controlling
and spiritualizing the body, the soul is [then] controlled by
it."[28] In the formation of girls and young women, it is especially important that emotional stirrings be placed under the
control of reason and the direction of the will. "Where discipline of the mind and will are lacking, emotional life becomes
compulsion without secure direction",[29] Edith Stein warns.

Before the Fall, man and woman were created to comple-
ment one another. Woman's interest in other persons com-
plements man's interest in things and in his projects, for it is
her particular joy to find her interest in a person and to be

[27] Ibid., p. 48.
[28] Ibid., p. 95.
[29] Ibid., p. 97.

interested in his concerns for his sake. Since the Fall, this complementarity includes helping one another to overcome or
avoid typical faults. In the raising of children, man and woman
must compensate for one another's shortcomings. The man
may have the tendency to provide well for the children, but
in an impersonal way. The woman, on the other hand, may
become overly attached to her children, tending to hover
anxiously over them and treating them as though they were
her possessions. The man helps his wife to be more objective and to focus on the discipline needed for work, while the
wife helps her husband to keep his focus on persons, so that
he does not become one-sided or lose himself in his work.

Edith Stein beautifully describes the ideal qualities of the
feminine soul:

> The soul of woman must therefore be *expansive* and open
> to all human beings; it must be *quiet* so that no small weak
> flame will be extinguished by stormy winds; *warm* so as not
> to benumb fragile buds; *clear*, so that no vermin will settle
> in dark corners and recesses; *self-contained*, so that no inva-
> sions from without can imperil the inner life; *empty of itself*, in
> order that extraneous life may have room in it; finally, *mistress
> of itself* and also of its body, so that the entire person is readily
> at the disposal of every call.[30]

Woman's soul is first of all to be *expansive*; that is, it is to
have room in it for others. The natural feminine empathy

---

[30] Stein, "Fundamental Principles of Women's Education", in *Essays on
Woman*, pp. 132–33.

and interest in the person is to be directed *toward* the other and *for* the other. With the help of grace, this expansiveness is expressed as a tactful, loving empathy and interest that embraces the other, seeking to help and to shelter him.

In order to respond to others, and especially in order to respond to invitations of grace, the feminine soul must be *quiet*. This quiet is not a mere lack of noise, but an active attentiveness to God and to others that includes a silencing of one's own plans and desires. Only insofar as the quietness of the soul is a turning *toward* God and toward the needs of others is it a virtue. The feminine soul, which is *warm* by its nature, is then able to bring this warmth to other souls. This warmth is inconstant unless it is nourished by divine grace.

There are many reports of Sister Teresa Benedicta's quiet way and warm, yet reserved, goodness. Before she entered Carmel, her expansive heart became visible primarily in two ways: in her generous aid to the poor and in the attention and the time she gave to her students and to all who called upon her when she was teaching in Speyer. Especially around Christmas, the busy teacher provided gifts for the poor of the city.[31] Because she lived in austere poverty, she could be generous with the poor. Witnesses to Edith's charity attest: "God alone knows how many people she helped, counseled

[31] See Teresia Renata Posselt, O.C.D., *Edith Stein: Eine Grosse Frau unseres Jahrhunderts*, 9th ed. (Freiburg: Herder, 1963), p. 73, quoting a young teacher at Speyer: "There were always great goings-on in her room before Christmas. There was a surprise for everyone in any way connected with her, all beautifully wrapped up. And what big parcels found their way secretly to the poor in the town! I do not know how she got hold of the addresses for it. It was the Sister who looked after her room who told me about it."

and guided as an angel of mercy in spiritual and material cri-
ses. There were often many claims on her attention and an
extensive correspondence to be maintained, yet she always
found time to meet new requests."[32]

Edith emphasizes that helping others must be determined
by God's will: one "may approach them only if one is *sent* to
them",[33] she says. There is a strong element of tactful reserve
and a gentleness of approach that governed Edith Stein's
charity. The Dominican Sisters of Speyer report that "she
had a good eye for opportunities of giving welcome assistance where it had not even been asked",[34] so that she would,
for example, help in the kitchen after meals on high feast days
so that the sisters could all participate in recreation.[35]

Edith's tactful reserve, together with her warmth, made
others feel safe with her. One of her former students in
Speyer wrote: "In my compositions, I felt able to express
my personal opinions and my intimate feelings without any
hesitation, knowing that only she would read them. I was
convinced that I could say absolutely anything, be totally

[32] Quoted in Herbstrith, *Edith Stein*, p. 78. For a slightly different English
translation, see: Sister Teresia Renata Posselt, O.C.D., *Edith Stein: The Life of
a Philosopher and Carmelite*, p. 67. Cf. *Kölner Selig- und Heiligsprechungsprozess*,
p. 43, no. 54: "Her door was always open for those who sought counsel and
assistance, and she dedicated herself to them with all the affection of her heart."

[33] Stein, "Fundamental Principles of Women's Education", in *Essays on
Woman*, p. 133.

[34] Quoted in Posselt, *Edith Stein: The Life of a Philosopher and Carmelite*, p. 67.

[35] See Posselt, *Edith Stein: The Life of a Philosopher and Carmelite*, p. 67. Cf.
Kölner Selig- und Heiligsprechungsprozess, p. 43, no. 54: "On Sundays and feast
days, she was just as willing to substitute for the Sisters in the kitchen to wash
dishes and to clean up, so that the Sisters could participate in their common
recreation."

honest and open, without being misunderstood."[36] Whatever a person told her was safe with her. Fifteen years after
her death, the Cologne Carmel received a letter from a superior writing about difficulties in her monastery. In the letter,
the superior assumed that Sister Teresa Benedicta, to whom
she had written about the situation many years earlier, had
told her own superiors about it. This was not the case. She
had never said or suggested anything negative about other
convents.[37]

The quietness of her soul allowed Edith Stein to be wholly
present to God, especially during times of prayer. In this
spirit, she was able to accept His will, even when it meant
her deportation and martyrdom. When Mr. Alois Schlütter
saw her at the deportation camp and wished her the best,
the Carmelite responded that he "need not worry about her,
she is in God's Hand".[38] Only the quiet soul, the soul not
noisily filled with its own wishes, worries, and plans, can so
calmly embrace God's will. Quiet herself, she was able to
recognize and to attend to the needs of others at the camp:

[36] Quoted in Herbstrith, *Edith Stein*, p. 77. For a slightly different English
translation, see Posselt, *Edith Stein: The Life of a Philosopher and Carmelite*, p. 71.

[37] See *Kölner Selig- und Heiligsprechungsprozess*, p. 60, no. 74: "In the same
way, she practiced moderation in communicating what others had confided to
her. Here is one example of how she did this in practice: Fifteen years after her
death, the Cologne Carmel received a letter, in which the superior of a convent
expressed her serious concerns. The author assumed that the Servant of God
had told her superior in Carmel about these concerns. That, however, was not
the case. Edith Stein had never said, not even suggested, an unfavorable word
about other convents."

[38] Report of Mr. Alois Schlütter of May 1, 1949 about his and Mr. Philipsen's
visit in Westerbork, in *Kölner Selig- und Heiligsprechungsprozess*, p. 23, no. 26.

she looked after the children—washing them, feeding them, playing with them—when their own mothers were too distraught to do so.[39]

Implications for Careers

Given the differences between man and woman, Edith Stein inquires whether there are particularly masculine or particularly feminine vocations and careers. Is there something inherently disordered about a woman who works on a construction site, or is it consonant with her feminine nature?

There certainly are, Edith Stein asserts, careers that are more naturally suited to men and ones more suited to women. It may well be true today, as it was in the 1930s, that many people must accept work for which they are by nature unsuited, because no other work is available. In such cases, "there is nothing left but to make the most of the situation: the pertinent professional requirements must be satisfied but not at the cost of denying one's own nature by permitting it to atrophy."[40]

---

[39] See ibid., p. 45, no. 58: "Her perfect charity shone in its brightest lustre, however, in the Concentration Camp of Westerbork. While most of the women there cried and lamented, or wrangled with God and their fate, she was like an Angel of Peace to all around her. She consoled, encouraged, and helped everyone around her. She had so fully forgotten herself and her own threatening situation that she could even play and joke with the children, in order to cheer them up a little, after they had been intimidated and neglected by their mothers who had become apathetic from the pain."

[40] Stein, "The Separate Vocations of Man and Woman according to Nature and Grace", in *Essays on Woman*, p. 82.

Masculine careers usually require physical strength, an ability to think abstractly, and independent creativity in fields such as agriculture, industry, and technology. Masculine professions involve working with inanimate things and with abstract concepts. A man who is forced to accept an unsuitable job can make it more harmonious with his masculine nature by exercising his inventive creativity.

Feminine qualities are needed when feeling, intuition, empathy, and adaptability come into play. Activities that involve caring for the *total* person are particularly suitable for women. Edith Stein says that feminine professions include

> [those] depending on sympathetic rapport such as nursing, education, and social work; consequently, also included would be the vocation of doctor and nurse, teacher and governess, housemaid, and the entire range of contemporary social services. In scholarship it would be those branches dealing with the concrete, living personal element, i.e., the arts and positions wherein one may help and serve, such as translating, editing, and, possibly, guiding a stranger's work appreciatively.[41]

Even professions that would not seem to be harmonious with the feminine nature can be practiced in an authentically feminine way. In almost every job, there is contact with other people, and this gives a ready opportunity to practice feminine virtues. When a woman, contrary to her natural

---

[41] Stein, "The Ethos of Women's Professions", in *Essays on Woman*, p. 49.

inclination, is required to perform work that is more suited to the masculine nature, Edith Stein counsels that

> an adjustment to dull material or abstract thought is demanded, as in work in a factory, business office, national or municipal service, legislature, chemical laboratory or mathematical institute. But in most instances, the work is conducted with other people, at least with others in the same room; often it is a division of labor. And with it an immediate opportunity is given for development of all feminine virtues. One can even say that the development of the feminine nature can become a blessed counterbalance precisely here where everyone is in danger of becoming mechanized and losing his humanity.[42]

When asked whether a woman should remain primarily in the home, Edith Stein, writing in the early 1930s, responded as follows:

> On the whole does woman's professional life outside of the home violate the order of nature and grace? I believe that one must answer "no" to this question.... Wherever the circle of domestic duties is too narrow for the wife to attain the full formation of her powers, both nature and reason concur that she reach out beyond this circle. It appears to me, however, that there is a limit to such professional activities whenever it jeopardizes domestic life, i.e., the community of life and formation consisting of parents and children.[43]

[42] Ibid., p. 50.
[43] Stein, "The Separate Vocations of Man and Woman according to Nature and Grace", in *Essays on Woman*, pp. 79–80.

On the other hand, though, she writes that "we should accept as normal that the married woman is restricted to domestic life at a time when her household duties exact her total energies."[44]

Edith Stein presents a well-balanced view of the differences between man and woman. Since both men and women are *persons*, they ought to have the same rights: the right to an education, the right to vote, the right to choose their professions. A woman will be at peace with herself and others only if she fully develops her feminine qualities; a man will be at peace with himself and others only if he fully develops his masculine qualities. Both men and women are essential in building up the Mystical Body of Christ, and it is in acceptance of our God-given sex with its characteristic strengths and weaknesses that we begin to accept God's will for our lives.

[44] Ibid., p. 80.

4

Communion with God's Will

Much as we may like to think that we are in control of our lives, there are many realities that we do not choose and must accept as God's will: we do not choose our place of birth or our family; we do not choose the particular crosses and challenges that mark our personality and the course of our life. Many of the joys and sorrows we face in life are not chosen, but received.

In a society in which freedom is exalted and is often understood as freedom *from* authority—as freedom from rules and regulations, as freedom to do as I please—it is more difficult for us to be convinced that our true happiness lies not in doing what we please, but in doing what pleases our heavenly Father. Following God's will for us, not merely in following the Ten Commandments, but also in being attentive to His will in following the state in life to which He calls us, and especially in doing His will in small, everyday affairs, is what will make us of "one heart and one soul" with our Lord and will bring us unspeakable peace and joy.

When she talks about doing God's will, Edith Stein speaks of following our God-given vocation. Hearing the word *vocation*, we may think first of the priesthood and consecrated life, while knowing that marriage and the single life are also vocations. Edith Stein often uses the word *vocation* in an even broader sense to include our profession or our work, since, she says, God has created us for and called us to some specific work. Edith counsels laypeople who must choose their own work to make sure that their choice is not a merely human decision. Always realistic, Edith acknowledges that it is not always possible to do the work that one believes God has called him to do.[1]

The Role of the Spiritual Director

Our sex, says Edith Stein, is one factor that helps us to know the type of work to which God calls us, as was considered in chapter 3. Another way that we come to know God's will—even with respect to our profession—is through following the counsel of a spiritual director. A spiritual director can be especially important for the layperson, who is not under obedience to a bishop or a religious superior. One way of ascertaining God's will, Edith notes, "comes from obedience shown to a visible proxy of God—a priestly director. According to everything which we learn from personal experience and the history of salvation, the Lord's method is to form persons through other persons. Just as the child is assigned to the

[1] See Stein, "The Separate Vocations of Man and Woman according to Nature and Grace", in *The Collected Works of Edith Stein*, vol. 2, *Essays on Woman*, trans. Freda Mary Oben, ed. L. Gelber and R. Leuven, O.C.D., 2nd rev. ed. (Washington, D.C.: ICS Publications, 1996), p. 82.

care and upbringing of an adult for his natural development, so also is the life of grace propagated through human mediation."[2] In order to stay on the right path of God's will, "there is no better protection than obedience toward an enlightened religious director. It is a *mysterious* fact that obedience is efficacious against the powers of darkness ... but it is a *fact*."[3]

By submitting to a spiritual director, Edith Stein explains, we avoid mistaking our own will for God's will. Given our fallen human nature, we tend to divinize our own will. In order to protect ourselves from this tendency, "it is good to make decisions by submitting oneself to calm, unbiased judgment rather than by just following one's inner promptings. Another fact to be considered", she adds, "is that judgment in one's own affairs tends to be less certain and reliable than it is for others."[4]

Submission to the will of another is not a sign of weakness or indecision; it is rather a sign of strength and conviction. Obedience did not come naturally to Edith. In a letter to Roman Ingarden, written before her conversion, she writes the following about her work as an assistant to Professor Edmund Husserl:

I can place myself at the service of something, and I can do all manner of things for the love of someone, but to be at the service of a person, in short—to obey, is something I cannot do. And if Husserl will not accustom himself once more to

[2] Stein, "Spirituality of the Christian Woman", in *Essays on Woman*, pp. 126–27.
[3] Ibid., p. 127.
[4] Ibid.

treat me as a collaborator in the work—as I have always considered our company to be and he, in theory, did likewise—
then we shall have to part company.[5]

Once baptized, Edith Stein wanted to become a Carmelite
nun.[6] Given her determination and strength of will, one would
have expected her to enter Carmel immediately, despite the
obstacles. Her spiritual director at the time, Canon Joseph
Schwind, however, counseled against her entrance.[7] He suggested that, rather than entering the cloister, she should teach

[5] Stein to Roman Ingarden, February 2, 1918, in *The Collected Works of Edith
Stein*, vol. 5, *Edith Stein: Self-Portrait in Letters*, trans. Sister Josephine Koeppel,
O.C.D., ed. L. Gelber and R. Leuven, O.C.D. (Washington, D.C.: ICS Pub-
lications, 1993), no. 19, p. 22. Edith Stein did, in fact, "part company" with
Dr. Husserl. Only twenty days after the above-quoted letter, she wrote to
Roman Ingarden that "the Master has graciously accepted my resignation" (see
Stein to Roman Ingarden, February 28, 1918, in ibid., no. 20, p. 23). Other
examples of Edith Stein's determination and strong self-will include her rejec-
tion of the Jewish faith at the age of fourteen and her insistence on serving as
a nurse in the First World War, despite her mother's staunch opposition (see
The Collected Works of Edith Stein, vol. 1, *Life in a Jewish Family*, pp. 318–19).

[6] See Stein, "How I Came to the Cologne Carmel", in Sister Teresia Renata
Posselt, O.C.D., *Edith Stein: The Life of a Philosopher and Carmelite*, ed. Susanne
M. Batzdorff, Sister Josephine Koeppel, O.C.D., and Reverend John Sullivan, O.C.D. (Washington, D.C.: ICS Publications, 2005), p. 118: "For almost
twelve years, Carmel had been my goal; since summer 1921 when the *Life* of
our Holy Mother Teresa had happened to fall into my hands and had put an
end to my long search for the true faith. When on New Year's Day 1922, I
received the Sacrament of Baptism, I thought that this was merely the preparation for entering the Order."

[7] It is true that Edith Stein herself also recognized that it would be better to
wait to enter Carmel. She says that "when for the first time since my baptism I
stood face to face with my dear mother, it became clear to me that she would
not be able to withstand this second blow [of Edith's entrance into Carmel]
for the time being. She would not die of it, but it would fill her with such
bitterness that I could not take the responsibility for that. I would have to wait
patiently" (ibid., p. 118).

at Saint Magdalene teachers' training college in Speyer, where she would be able to live quietly near the convent and grow in her Catholic Faith, particularly through the study of the works of Saint Thomas Aquinas.[8] Edith Stein obeyed. Having aspired to being a professor in a university, taking on a position in a teachers' training college must have been a disappointment for her on the human level; but in her writing we find no hint of such disappointment, and we may suppose that she accepted her spiritual director's advice as God's will for her.

During the eight years that Edith taught at Saint Magdalene, from 1923 to 1931, she learned to live her Catholic Faith deeply. Although she was not a religious sister, she lived as though she were in the convent, practicing extreme simplicity and taking private vows of poverty, chastity, and obedience. She continued in her teaching position until her new spiritual director, whom she had sought out after Canon Schwind's death, Archabbot Raphael Walzer, O.S.B., suggested that she stop teaching and give lectures throughout Germany. She who longed for the seclusion and silence of the cloister was now to travel throughout Europe as a lecturer. The Acts of the Process of Beatification and Canonization suggest how difficult this obedience must have been for her: "And Edith Stein submitted, even if with a bleeding heart."[9] The same

[8] See *Kölner Selig- und Heiligsprechungsprozess der Dienerin Gottes Sr. Teresia Benedicta a Cruce (Edith Stein): Professe und Chorschwester des Ordens der Allerseligsten Jungfrau Maria vom Berge Karmel* (Cologne: Kloster der Karmelitinnen "Maria vom Frieden", 1962), p. 8, no. 10: "Since she had an intense longing for the silence of the cloister, he [Father Schwind, Vicar General of Speyer] offered to find a quiet little place where she could dedicate herself without interruption to her academic work and, at the same time, she could continue her religious development."

[9] Ibid., p. 10, no. 13.

Acts do not hesitate to qualify her obedience to her spiritual director as *heroic*: "In the spirit of faith she submitted heroically, despite her intense desire for Carmel, to the decision of her spiritual director, confident that she was thus fulfilling God's will."[10]

When the anti-Semitic laws in Germany made it impossible for Edith Stein to continue her apostolate, she saw therein God's will. After spending time in prayer on Good Shepherd Sunday of 1933, Edith was certain that it was God's will that she enter Carmel. She writes that, "after the concluding blessing had been pronounced, I had the assurance of the Good Shepherd."[11] Even though she felt certain of God's will for her, she did not proceed with her plan until she had the approval of her spiritual director. Since Archabbot Walzer was, in fact, abroad, she had to wait some weeks before she received his permission to make initial contact with the Carmel in Cologne.

Edith Stein herself carried out informal spiritual direction with various persons, especially with her students and the young religious sisters at Speyer. Erna Hermann first met Edith in 1931 and was later a student at the teachers' college in Speyer. Edith was Erna's confirmation sponsor. When she was a student in Speyer, Erna once invited Edith for a social visit. In her written response to the invitation, Edith wrote: "During all these years in Speyer, I have never fostered any social life involving mutual visits. Anyone familiar with my commitments will not hold this against me. Many people come to me and everyone who comes, hoping to find some help from me, is heartily welcome. Obviously, that also holds for you, and I should no longer need to assure you of this."[12]

Some months after writing this letter, Edith sent Erna a letter with some spiritual advice. She wrote:

> I would also like to send you a small decoration for your room as a Christmas greeting. Of course, were it in my power, I would much rather give you something else, something far more beautiful: the true childlike spirit that opens the door to the approaching Savior, that can say from the heart—not theoretically but practically in each and every case—"Lord, not mine, but thy will be done." I am telling you this because I would like to help you attain the one thing necessary. In the past months I have often been concerned because, repeatedly, I had the impression that there is still something lacking on this most important point, that an obstinate self-will is present, a tenacious clinging to desires once conceived. And if I have seemed to you, perhaps, hard and relentless because I would not give in to your wishes, then believe me, that was not due to coldness or a lack of love, but because of a firm conviction that I should harm you by acting otherwise. I am only a tool of the Lord. I would like to lead to him anyone who comes to me. And when I notice that this is not the case, but that the interest is invested in my person, then I cannot serve as a tool and must beg the Lord to help in other ways. After all, he is never dependent on only one

[12] Stein to Erna Hermann, September 16, 1930, in Stein, *Self-Portrait in Letters*, no. 63, p. 68.

individual. Won't you make use of these last days of Advent
for an honest self-examination, so that you will be granted a
truly grace-filled Christmas?[13]

Edith Stein's words may seem severe, but they reveal that
she never separated love from truth, and they remind us
of Pope Benedict XVI's words, already mentioned above:
"*Only in truth does charity shine forth*, only in truth can charity be authentically lived.... Without truth, charity degen-
erates into sentimentality. Love becomes an empty shell."[14]
Edith's charity was always rooted in the truth. She did not
seek human respect, she did not seek to be loved, but she
loved purely, seeking the good of Erna's soul.[15] Her words
reveal that Edith recognized that seeking and knowing God's
will are essential in the spiritual life.

Graces from One's State of Life

Living in communion with God's will consists not only in
embracing our God-given vocation (our state of life *and* our
profession), but also in the daily living out of that vocation.
Being faithful is a daily challenge. There are struggles in every
vocation, and it is easy to become downcast or disheartened.
Edith Stein describes the challenge faced by working mothers

[13] Stein to Erna Hermann, December 19, 1930, in ibid., no. 76, p. 77.

[14] Benedict XVI, *Caritas in Veritate* (Vatican City State: Libreria Editrice Vaticana, 2009), no. 3.

[15] Cf. *Kölner Selig- und Heiligsprechungsprozess*, p. 56, no. 72: "All forms of
human respect were foreign to her. She never spoke or acted to please others,
and she never neglected to do good, even if it were to turn out to her own
harm."

as one example of challenges we may encounter: "Many of the best women are almost overwhelmed by the double burden of family duties and professional life—or often simply of only gainful employment. Always on the go, they are harassed, nervous, and irritable. Where are they to get the inner peace and cheerfulness in order to offer stability, support, and guidance to others?"[16]

How can we live our God-given vocation in the way that God would have us live it? Our lives are so busy; we become so tired; we face so many problems. Each state in life has a special source of help. Married persons, Edith Stein counsels, ought to rely on the real and ever-present grace conferred by the sacrament of matrimony.[17] She describes the power of grace in the life of a married woman:

> She is strengthened by grace for her vocation, as long as she does her utmost to remain a living member of the Church and to lead a married life in the sense of the Church. And even with an unworthy spouse who makes her life an ordeal, even in this terrible distortion of the marriage ideal, the woman will be able to persevere in the marriage bond if she still honors the metaphor of the mystical life.[18]

Both priests and religious, says Edith Stein, have as the essence of their vocation a total surrender to the Lord and a bridal relationship. The religious woman is espoused to Christ; the priest, as another Christ, is espoused to the Church. It is this

[16] Stein, "The Ethos of Women's Professions", in *Essays on Woman*, p. 54.
[17] Stein, "Spirituality of the Christian Woman", in *Essays on Woman*, p. 121.
[18] Ibid., p. 122.

surrender that gives priests and religious the strength to fulfill their vocation. Religious, moreover, find their support in their community.[19]

In one of her lectures on the spirituality of the Christian woman, Edith Stein speaks at length about the vocation of the single person. Where, she inquires, can such a person find strength for living his vocation? She notes that some single persons are such because they had to renounce marriage, even though they felt attracted to it, or because they were unable to enter religious life when they wanted to do so. Often the single life is not as much a chosen vocation as a vocation that circumstances have forced upon the person. When the single life is not freely chosen, there is a danger, Edith Stein says, that the single woman (as well as the single man) "views her life as a failure, that her soul becomes stunted and embittered, that it does not provide the strength for her to function fruitfully as a woman".[20]

The single person will find strength for living his vocation by seeing God's will at work in the circumstances and by embracing His will. Once the single person surrenders to God's will, then God will surely grant special graces of guidance.

The Holy Eucharist and Prayer

In addition to the sources of strength that we find in our state of life, the Holy Sacrifice of the Mass and Holy Communion,

[19] See ibid., pp. 122–23.
[20] Ibid., p. 124.

as well as our daily prayers, are necessary sources of grace that enable us to do God's will. We meet people from every walk of life who perform their duties well, are always generous with their time, and are kind and warm. Seeing such people, we may ask: "What is the source of their strength? How [to] explain all their achievements which one might often declare to be impossible by nature? How [to] account for that unruffled peace and cheerfulness even in the keenest nervous and emotional stress?"[21]

The answer, says Edith Stein, is simple: Christ and His eucharistic presence provide these people with supernatural strength and grace. We can fulfill God's will joyfully each day—we can remain generous, kind, and peaceful in the midst of all life's difficulties, problems, and obstacles—if we turn daily to our eucharistic Lord, receive Him often in Holy Communion, and live in communion with Him. We must allow Him to live in us. Edith Stein explains:

> For every Catholic there lies ready an immeasurable treasure: the proximity of the Lord in the holy sacrifice and in the most holy sacrament of the altar. Whoever is imbued with a lively faith in Christ present in the tabernacle, whoever knows that a friend awaits here constantly—always with the time, patience, and sympathy to listen to complaints, petitions, and problems, with counsel and help in all things—this person cannot remain desolate and forsaken even under the greatest difficulties. He always has a refuge where quietude and peace can again be found.

[21] Stein, "The Ethos of Women's Professions", in *Essays on Woman*, p. 56.

And whoever is penetrated by the meaning of the sacrifice of the Mass, it were as if he had grown into Christ's
redemptive action. The small and great offerings asked of
him daily are no longer compulsory, inflicted, overwhelming
burdens. Rather, they become true sacrifices, freely and joyfully offered, through which he wins a share in the work of
redemption as a co-suffering member of the Mystical Body
of Christ.[22]

After Edith Stein's conversion "the Reverend [Joseph]
Schwind had introduced her to the liturgical year and had
taught her to pray the Breviary, which she daily fulfilled
from then on with iron fidelity."[23] From the time of her
baptism, Edith also assisted daily at Holy Mass and received

---

[22] Stein, "Spirituality of the Christian Woman", in *Essays on Woman*,
pp. 120–21. See also p. 125: "It is most important that the Holy Eucharist
becomes life's focal point: that the Eucharistic Savior is the center of existence;
that every day is received from His hand and laid back therein; that the day's
happenings are deliberated with Him. In this way, God is given the best opportunity to be heard in the heart, to form the soul, and to make its faculties clear-
sighted and alert for the supernatural. It then comes about of itself that one sees
the problems of one's own life with God's eyes and that one learns to resolve
them in His spirit. For this, a peaceful and clear-headed consideration of exterior facts and events must emerge. Whoever lives in the strong faith that nothing happens without the knowledge and will of God is not easily disconcerted
by astonishing occurrences or upset by the hardest of blows. He will stay quiet
and face the facts clearly; he will discover the right guidelines for his practical
behavior in the overall situation. Moreover, life with the Eucharistic Savior
induces the soul to be lifted out of the narrowness of its individual, personal
orbit. The concerns of the Lord and His kingdom become the soul's concerns."

[23] *Kölner Selig- und Heiligsprechungsprozess*, p. 8, no. 11. Edith Stein's commitment to praying the full Breviary, in addition to her many obligations in
the world, is even more notable when one considers that the prayers of the
Breviary prior to the changes introduced by Pope Paul VI in 1974 were signifi-
cantly longer than those of the Breviary that has been in use since 1974.

the sacrament of penance once a week.[24] Knowing that the reception of Holy Communion is the highest of all goods, she allowed no obstacle to prevent her from receiving it daily. At the Process of her Beatification and Canonization it was pointed out that, "even if so many obstacles and pressing reasons stood in the way, as was often the case on her long journeys to give lectures, no exertion, no inconvenience could keep her from assisting at Holy Mass and from receiving Holy Communion."[25] At that time, the reception of Holy Communion still required one to fast from midnight onward.

In addition to the Holy Sacrifice of the Mass and the reception of Holy Communion, personal prayer is an important source of strength. Even before her entrance into Carmel, many noted Edith Stein's fidelity to prayer. She often spent the days of the Holy Triduum at the Benedictine Abbey of Beuron, and "eye-witnesses report that for hours on end she knelt there unmoved, sunk in deep prayer in the abbey church."[26] She would kneel for hours without interruption, never sitting, out of reverence for our eucharistic Lord.[27]

[24] See ibid., p. 49, no. 64: "Weekly reception of the Sacrament of Penance and her daily nourishment through the Holy Eucharist were a self-understood aspect of her love of Christ."

[25] Ibid., p. 26, no. 33.

[26] Letter of Frau Kath. Schreier of August 21, 1947, in *Kölner Selig- und Heiligsprechungsprozess*, p. 10, no. 13.

[27] Cf. *Kölner Selig- und Heiligsprechungsprozess*, p. 26, no. 33: "Her reverence for the Real Presence of Christ under the appearance of bread did not permit her to take up any other position in Church but kneeling. Very often, especially in the Abbey of Beuron, she knelt for many hours. She knelt without interruption and she seemed not to tire at all of praying." Regarding her comportment in Carmel, see also ibid., pp. 74–75, no. 96: "When it was at all possible, then, on the Feast of Corpus Christi she remained from morning until evening kneeling on the bare floor in adoration before the exposed Monstrance."

In one of her lectures, Edith Stein describes in an emi-
nently practical way the importance of personal prayer and
explains how we can find time for prayer in our busy lives. I
quote her at length:

> The duties and cares of the day ahead crowd about us when
> we awake in the morning (if they have not already dispelled
> our night's rest). Now arises the uneasy question: How can
> all this be accommodated in one day? When will I do this,
> when that? How shall I start on this and that? Thus agitated,
> we would like to run around and rush forth. We must then
> take the reins in hand and say, "Take it easy! Not any of this
> may touch me now. My first morning's hour belongs to the
> Lord. I will tackle the day's work which He charged me
> with, and He will give me the power to accomplish it."
>
> So I will go to the altar of God. Here it is not a question of
> my minute, petty affairs, but of the great offering of recon-
> ciliation. I may participate in that, purify myself and be made
> happy, and lay myself with all my doings and troubles along
> with the sacrifice on the altar. And when the Lord comes to
> me in Holy Communion, then I may ask Him, "Lord, what
> do you want of me?" (St. Teresa). And after quiet dialogue, I
> will go to that which I see as my next duty.
>
> I will still be joyful when I enter into my day's work after
> this morning's celebration: my soul will be empty of that
> which could assail and burden it, but it will be filled with
> holy joy, courage, and energy.
>
> Because my soul has left itself and entered into the divine
> life, it has become great and expansive. Love burns in it like
> a composed flame which the Lord has enkindled, and which
> urges my soul to render love and to inflame love in others:

"*flammescat igne caritas, accendat ardor proximos.*" And it sees clearly the next part of the path before it; it does not see very far, but it knows that when it has arrived at that place where the horizon now intersects, a new vista will then be opened.

Now begins the day's work, perhaps the teaching profession—four or five hours, one after the other. That means giving our concentration there. We cannot achieve in each hour what we want, perhaps in none. We must contend with our own fatigue, unforeseen interruptions, shortcomings of the children, diverse vexations, indignities, anxieties. Or perhaps it is office work: give and take with disagreeable supervisors and colleagues, unfulfilled demands, unjust reproaches, human meanness, perhaps also distress of the most distinct kind.

It is the noon hour. We come home exhausted, shattered. New vexations possibly await there. Now where is the soul's morning freshness? The soul would like to seethe and storm again: indignation, chagrin, regret. And there is still so much to do until evening. Should we not go immediately to it? No, not before calm sets in at least for a moment. Each one must know, or get to know, where and how she can find peace. The best way, when it is possible, is to shed all cares again for a short time before the tabernacle. Whoever cannot do that, whoever also possibly requires bodily rest, should take a breathing space in her own room. And when no outer rest whatever is attainable, when there is no place in which to retreat, if pressing duties prohibit a quiet hour, then at least she must for a moment seal off herself inwardly against all other things and take refuge in the Lord. He is indeed there and can give us in a single moment what we need.

Thus the remainder of the day will continue, perhaps in great fatigue and laboriousness, but in peace. And when night comes, and retrospect shows that everything was patchwork and much which one had planned left undone, when so many things rouse shame and regret, then take all as it is, lay it in God's hands, and offer it up to Him. In this way we will be able to rest in Him, actually to rest, and to begin the new day like a new life.

This is only a small indication how the day could take shape in order to make room for God's grace. Each individual will best know how this can be used in her particular circumstances. It could be further indicated how Sunday must be a great door through which celestial life can enter into everyday life, and strength for the work of the entire week, and how the great feasts, holidays, and the seasons of Lent, lived through in the spirit of the Church, permit the soul to mature the more from year to year to the eternal Sabbath rest.[28]

Childlike Confidence

The last practical suggestion Edith Stein offers for living in harmony with God's will is fostering a childlike trust in His providence. In this childlike attitude she followed her Carmelite sister Saint Thérèse of the Child Jesus and the Holy Face.[29] In one of her letters, Sister Teresa Benedicta counsels:

[28] Edith Stein, "Fundamental Principles of Women's Education", in *Essays on Woman*, pp. 143–45.

[29] At first consideration, Sister Teresa Benedicta of the Cross and her Carmelite sister Saint Thérèse seem quite dissimilar. Saint Thérèse entered Carmel at the tender age of fifteen, after having been raised in a devoutly Catholic family. She spent nearly all her life before entering the convent in the small circle of her family in a provincial town and obtained no higher education. Saint

"Lay all care for the future, confidently, in God's hands, and allow yourself to be led by him entirely, as a child would. Then you can be sure not to lose your way."[30] In a letter to a religious sister, Edith Stein explains that, in all her lectures, "it is always a small, simple truth that I have to express: *How to go about living at the Lord's hand*."[31] In the same letter, she explains that when she was asked to give lectures on various topics, she could use those topics only as an introduction to this one theme. Showing people how to go about living at the Lord's hand had become Edith Stein's consuming theme, so that she could speak of nothing else.

It is not childish to have utter confidence in God. Trusting completely in God's providence is most reasonable; fearing about our future and failing to trust our heavenly Father is unreasonable. Reminding us of Saint Thérèse, Sister Teresa Benedicta writes: "I am conscious of being held and in this knowledge I have peace and security—not the self-assured security of the persons who stand on safe ground due to their own strength, but the sweet and blessed security of the child supported by a strong arm—a security which, from a

---

Teresa Benedicta pursued advanced studies before converting to Catholicism. Once a Catholic, she taught for many years and then began to give public lectures throughout Europe. While Saint Thérèse entered the cloister before the usual age, Saint Teresa Benedicta entered much later than most. Despite these differences, not to mention the differences in their personalities, the spiritual lives of both are marked by a childlike confidence in God.

[30] Sister Teresa Benedicta to Ruth Kantorowitz, October 4, 1934, in Stein, *Self-Portrait in Letters*, no. 181, p. 185.

[31] Stein to Sister Adelgundis Jaegerschmid, O.S.B., April 28, 1931, in ibid., no. 89, p. 87.

practical point of view, is no less sensible. Or would you call a child sensible who constantly lives in fear of being dropped by its mother?"[32]

Toward the end of her life, in the unfinished work *Finite and Eternal Being*, Sister Teresa Benedicta wrote, when giving an example of the causal nature of the world, that "what did not lie in *my* plan lay in *God's* plan. And the more often such things happen to me," she continued, "the more lively becomes in me the conviction of my faith that—from God's point of view—nothing is *accidental*, that my entire life, even in the most minute details, was pre-designed in the plans of divine providence and is thus for the all-seeing eye of God a perfect coherence of meaning [*Sinnzusammenhang*]."[33]

When we live by grace and in the presence of the Person of Christ, our emotional life is also changed, says Edith Stein. We see all in the light of Christ, and we feel joy and sorrow at that which causes Him joy and sorrow. In the end, she explains,

those who attain the freedom of these heights and expansive views have outgrown what is usually called "happiness" and "unhappiness". They may have to fight hard for worldly existence, may lack the support of a warm family life or, correspondingly, of the human community which sustains

[32] Edith Stein, *Finite and Eternal Being*, in *An Edith Stein Daybook: To Live at the Hand of the Lord*, trans. Susanne Batzdorff (Springfield, Ill.: Templegate Publishers, 1994), p. 12. For an alternative translation, see: *The Collected Works of Edith Stein*, vol. 9, *Finite and Eternal Being*, trans. Kurt F. Reinhardt, ed. L. Gelber and R. Leuven, O.C.D. (Washington, D.C.: ICS Publications, 2002), p. 58.

[33] Edith Stein, *Finite and Eternal Being*, p. 113.

and supports—but lonely and joyless they can no longer be. Those who live with Holy Church and its liturgy, i.e., as authentic Catholics, can never be lonely: they find themselves embedded in the great human community; everywhere, all are united as brothers and sisters in the depths of their hearts. And because streams of living water flow from all those who live in God's hand, they exert a mysterious magnetic appeal on thirsty souls. Without aspiring to it, they must become guides of other persons striving to the light; they must practice spiritual maternity, begetting and drawing sons and daughters nearer to the kingdom of God.[34]

[34] Stein, "Spirituality of the Christian Woman", in *Essays on Woman*, p. 126. Cf. Benedict XVI, Homily for Mass with Imposition of the Pallium and Conferral of the Fisherman's Ring for the Beginning of the Petrine Ministry of the Bishop of Rome (April 25, 2005): "Those who believe are never alone—neither in life nor in death."

5

School of Communion

In *Novo Millennio Ineunte*, Pope Saint John Paul II said that the spirituality of communion must be "the guiding principle of education".[1] It is not surprising that Christian education plays a key role in the new evangelization, in preparing young people to live according to the spirituality of communion as members of the Mystical Body of Christ.

In our day, even more so than nearly a century ago when Edith Stein spoke about the role of Christian education, the general conception of education is largely utilitarian. United States president Barack Obama, speaking about the importance of education, remarked: "A world-class education is the single most important factor in determining not just whether our kids can compete for the best jobs but whether America can out-compete countries around the world. America's business leaders understand that when it comes to education, we need to up our game. That's why we're

---

[1]John Paul II, Apostolic Letter *Novo Millennio Ineunte* (Boston: Pauline Books and Media, 2001), no. 43.

working together to put an outstanding education within reach for every child."[2] The purpose of education, then, according to the notion that President Obama articulated, is to find a good job, and good jobs are equated with well-paying jobs. A good education allows one to win in the jobs competition. President Obama was not presenting a new understanding of education but assumed that his conception is the usual one, as indeed it seems to be. This competitive notion of education does not promote the spirituality of communion, which seeks "to 'make room' for our brothers and sisters ... and [to resist] ... the selfish temptations which constantly beset us and provoke competition, careerism, distrust, and jealousy".[3]

The Catholic conception of education has never been merely utilitarian. The purpose of education is to prepare students to know and to do the good, to prepare them to know and embrace their vocation in life, and to form them in the spirituality of communion. The formation in the spirituality of communion is not merely one *aspect*

[2] Quoted in Ezra Mechaber, "Staying Competitive through Education: The President and American Business Leaders Announce New Commitments", *The White House Blog*, July 18, 2011, http://www.whitehouse.gov /blog/2011/07/18/staying-competitive-through-education-president-and -american-business-leaders-announ. Cf. Common Core State Standards Initiative mission statement: "The standards are designed to be robust and relevant to the real world, reflecting the knowledge and skills that our young people need for success in college and careers. With American students fully prepared for the future, our communities will be best positioned to compete successfully in the global economy" (http://www.learning.com/common core/ accessed October 12, 2014).

[3] John Paul II, *Novo Millennio Ineunte*, no. 43.

of education, but it is to be, as John Paul II says, *the guiding principle* of education.

The Catholic school, then, has a twofold task: education and formation. *Education* shapes the intellect and imparts practical knowledge, in both the natural and the supernatural order. Students are taught to read, to write, to know the Faith, and to be competent in various disciplines. Students also gain practical knowledge at school: from learning to use a pair of scissors in kindergarten to learning how to drive a car in high school.

Formation shapes character. Through the education received in school, students become certain types of persons, and the virtues they develop in school become formative of who they are. The formative role of the school is relevant to the theme of communion; for this reason, we will reflect solely upon this aspect of education in the present context.

The School of the Family

Both education and formation belong primarily to the family, not to the school; the parents are the child's primary educators. In the home, the young child learns to live in harmony with others and learns that he has a particular place and role in the community of the family. At home, the child will first come to know God and learn to love Him. Already in the early 1930s, Edith Stein observed that, with the collapse of the family, the role of education and formation began to fall more and more to the school. She wrote:

Where there is a sound family life and where the parents, especially the mother, really fulfill their vocation, the school's task will easily be one of wise restraint; it will not have much more to do than to reinforce the child's upbringing at home. But this is not the typical situation today. The destruction of family life has placed a greater responsibility on the school. Thus, it is correct if formation today is again considered as education's essential duty, and teaching as the method to achieve that goal.[4]

Before we consider what Edith Stein says about formation in the school, it may be worthwhile to dwell briefly on some of the things that she says about formation in the family. She emphasizes the role of the mother, because many of her lectures concern the role and vocation of women. In a lecture entitled "The Maternal Art of Formation", she begins by asking: "With what right should a woman [like herself], who herself is not a mother, dare to speak to mothers about the art of maternal formation?"[5] She replies that it is not primarily her study of psychology or of pedagogy but her vivid memory of her own childhood and her experience of seeing others raise their children that give her the authority to speak on the topic.

---

[4] Stein, "Spirituality of the Christian Woman", in *The Collected Works of Edith Stein*, vol. 2, *Essays on Woman*, trans. Freda Mary Oben, ed. L. Gelber and R. Leuven, O.C.D., 2nd rev. ed. (Washington, D.C.: ICS Publications, 1996), p. 113.

[5] Edith Stein, "Mütterliche Erziehungskunst", in *Edith Steins Werke*, vol. 12, *Ganzheitliches Leben: Schriften zur religiösen Bildung* (Freiburg: Herder, 1990), p. 151.

When we meet people who have a light and warm disposition, we can be almost certain, Edith Stein asserts, that they had a sunny childhood and that their mothers loved them in a healthy way. When, on the other hand, we meet people who are withdrawn and suspicious or who have other character defects, we can be equally sure that something went wrong in their childhood and, usually, that there was a failure in the mother's role.[6] Edith Stein underscores heavily the mother's role in formation.

In her presentation on the maternal art of formation, Edith Stein takes us through the stages of a child's life and underlines important ways in which a mother ought to form her child at each stage. The formation of the child's character is of the utmost importance, since our happiness depends not so much on our external circumstances as on our character.[7] Given that it is a weakness and a typical fault of a woman to become overly attached to and possessive of her children, it is of foremost importance for her to know and to impress upon herself that her child belongs to God and is not her property.

In preparation for the birth of a child, a mother must care for her physical well-being, but may not neglect her spiritual well-being. Her soul must be pure, so that her children will become good and happy. A mother must live a virtuous life because her example can have a helpful or harmful effect on her young child, even before the child can understand these impressions.

[6] See ibid., pp. 151–52.
[7] See ibid., p. 152.

The work of formation begins as soon as the child is born. Right from the start, Edith Stein counsels, there must be cleanliness and regularity in the baby's life. The baby needs to have regular feeding times and must become accustomed to that. If such regularity is wanting, Edith warns, the mother will soon have a little tyrant on her hands.

This cleanliness and regularity prepare the baby for obedience and orderliness. In the first years of life, the toddler must learn these two virtues. Although the child must have some freedom, he must also receive direction and obey. When the small child, whom Edith Stein calls "the little egoist",[8] realizes that crying or throwing a temper tantrum will cause his parents to change their commands or fail to carry out threatened consequences, the child will become, as she puts it, "the plague of the family",[9] and this will be to the child's own detriment.

As soon as the toddler begins to play with toys, it is time to form him in orderliness. Toys must be cleaned up and put away so that this becomes second nature to him. Edith Stein warns that, if this is not learned early on, it will be difficult to teach it later.

When the child begins to talk, the time has come to focus on the formation of truthfulness. A small child has difficulty in distinguishing reality from imagination, but he must learn the difference between the two, so that he can learn to distinguish truth from lies. Through the example of his parents, the child must learn to speak only the truth.

[8] Ibid., p. 154.
[9] Ibid.

All formation in the home must proceed from love, and when it does, the child will sense it. When formed in love, the child will grow up not to fear, but to trust others. The parents, moreover, must be living examples of all that they teach the child. The child's loving and trustful relationship with his parents is what will help him to relate to other persons. Of course, early on, the parents should introduce their child to the heavenly Father, so that the little one can learn to walk at the hand of God.

In the early years of the child's life, when the mother is home with him, the child is wholly in her hands. When it is time for him to go to school, many other influences will also contribute to his formation. For many children nowadays, the outside influence begins, sadly, much earlier at daycare centers. Since the school continues to form the young child, Edith stresses the importance of choosing a good school. She remarks that she is surprised how often parents send their children to a school without having made the effort to learn the spirit of the school and the principles that guide it. The school has a profound and lifelong effect on the child—for good or for ill.

The Role of the Teacher

The school, then, continues the work of formation. If the school is to form young people, we must know the goal of formation: Into what do we seek to form the children? Edith Stein describes the goal of formation in a lecture she gave on the role of religious sisters in the formation of children: "We must help to form the children of men into *children of God*. They ought to be *formed into God, formed into Christ*."[10] Children should learn to be led by God's will and to become living members of the Mystical Body of Christ. Formation has no small goal! Edith herself exclaims: "How frightening such a large task! But we may not settle for anything less."[11]

Children need to be *formed* into children of God. Although our fallen nature inclines us to selfishness, we are created for communion. In virtue of his baptism, each child already has supernatural life. God dwells in the child's soul, and the child is empowered by grace to live in harmony with God and with other persons. Baptism alone is not sufficient formation; the supernatural life is fragile, and it must be nurtured. Both the parents and the school must foster the child's life with God and allow it to develop.

Formation takes place on all levels of education, from the day care to the university. Edith Stein points out that, of all these, the elementary school is the most important place of formation. The elementary school teacher has the greatest influence on children since he is with the children for the entire day during their most formative years. Weighty is the responsibility of the teacher! Recognizing the daunting task of forming children into other Christs, a teacher may wonder

[10] Stein, "Die Mitwirkung der klösterlichen Bildungsanstalten an der religiösen Bildung der Jugend", in *Edith Stein Gesamtausgabe*, vol. 16, *Bildung und Entfaltung der Individualität: Beiträge zum christlichen Erziehungsauftrag*, ed. Sister Maria Amata Neyer, O.C.D., and Beate Beckmann-Zöller (Freiburg im Breisgau: Herder, 2001), p. 51.

[11] Ibid., p. 52.

how it can possibly be accomplished, particularly if he is not directly involved in the religious training of the students.

The teacher must not only know the Faith but must be permeated and transformed by it. Edith Stein remarks: "It makes a difference whether someone simply reports the facts of the Holy Scriptures as he would teach any other subject he has learned, or whether someone who was formed into His image through long, confident communication, and who is to a certain extent penetrated by Him, speaks of the Savior."[12] A teacher who lives with Christ intimately will know when and how to speak of Him in an appropriate way, also outside of religious instruction: "When the teacher, as a docile student, constantly attends the school of the Holy Scriptures, and allows the Savior to take him into *His* school, the children will notice that He is present, that He helps with the work; and in this way He grasps possession of their souls."[13]

Being formed by Christ does not mean that the teacher will turn every lesson into a religion class. Edith Stein warns that "nothing religious may ever be introduced in an artificial and external manner, and in a context where it has no place; otherwise, the children will feel that there is an 'ulterior motive,' and the effect, as a rule, is repellent instead of formative."[14] Mathematics class is not religion class.

It is not enough for the teacher to be another Christ, however. Every teacher, no matter what subject he teaches,

[12] Ibid., p. 54.
[13] Ibid.
[14] Ibid.

must also have a thorough *knowledge* of the Faith. When Edith Stein was teaching, she noticed that children often have questions about the Faith. At times they were afraid to ask their religion teacher and instead voiced their concerns in other classes. It is essential that the teacher be able to provide good and sound answers. "In order to find the right word, one's own strong faith alone is not always sufficient", Edith Stein maintains, and "an unsatisfactory answer can cause damage rather than help. For this reason thorough dogmatic knowledge is essential."[15] If children's doubts and questions are not properly addressed, they may easily reject the Faith altogether.

Always practical, Edith Stein realized that teachers will wonder how they can possibly find the time to study the Faith in order to gain such knowledge. The key is consistently to learn a little bit. Edith even suggests to religious sisters that, if there is other time available, they can use the time for daily meditation to learn more about the Faith; instead of using a devotional work for meditation, they could use the Holy Scriptures or a more dogmatic work.[16]

When writing to a religious sister who taught at a convent school, Edith Stein counseled that religious who serve as teachers "also need to know life as the children will find it. Otherwise", she writes, "there will be a great danger that the girls will tell themselves: 'The Sisters have no notion about the world'; 'They were unable to prepare us for the questions

---

[15] Ibid., p. 56.
[16] See ibid., pp. 56–57.

we now have to answer'; and the [danger] that then everything might be thrown overboard as useless."[17] In our day,
even more than in Edith Stein's day, children live in a society
that does not promote or support the Christian life. Teachers
need to know something of the challenges and temptations
that children will face in the world so that they can properly prepare their students to face them. Such preparation is
essential; without it, the children will have great difficulty in
sustaining their faith in the world.

Again and again, Edith Stein emphasizes that Christ in the
Holy Eucharist and in Holy Communion is the most powerful source of religious formation. Here, too, the teacher
must lead by example. At the time that Edith Stein wrote,
daily Holy Mass was the rule at most Catholic schools.
She says that students must sense that the teacher does not
attend Holy Mass simply because it is a rule, but because he
longs for it. Edith Stein provides a practical example of how
one can show that Christ in the Holy Mass is the center of
the day:

> If I were a principal, I would never arrange an excursion in
> such a way that the day would exclude Holy Mass and Com-
> munion. The joy and relaxation of the children need not be
> any less. If only one day is at one's disposal, then one does not
> let any thoughts arise of a distant excursion, but one chooses

[17] Stein to Sister Callista Kopf, October 20, 1932, in *The Collected Works
of Edith Stein*, vol. 5, *Edith Stein: Self-Portrait in Letters*, trans. Sister Josephine
Koeppel, O.C.D., ed. L. Gelber and R. Leuven, O.C.D. (Washington, D.C.:
ICS Publications, 1993), p. 122.

something nice nearby. If one meets with a spirited desire
for a more distant trip, then I think it appropriate to extend
it over two or more days rather than giving up the Highest
Good [i.e., Holy Mass] for it.[18]

When a teacher *lives* and *knows* the Faith, the children easily begin to love and to know Christ. The children must see,
in the life of the teacher, that the Faith is a source of joy and
peace. Then they will be drawn to it. In his task of bringing
the children to Christ, the teacher's role is like that of Saint
John the Baptist. The teacher leads the child to Christ. Once
the child arrives, the teacher may say with Saint John the
Baptist: "He must increase, but I must decrease."[19]

Formed into Community

The way that children in a classroom begin to know Jesus
and to become living members of His Mystical Body is by
becoming a community. They learn how to live with Christ
by learning to live in human communities. They learn to
find their place within the Mystical Body of Christ by finding
their role in the community of the classroom.

Life in community is necessary. Edith Stein asserts that
"*without community*, without the social life, and therefore,
without forming individuals into community members, *man's*

---

[18] Stein, "Die Mitwirkung der klösterlichen Bildungsanstalten an der
religiösen Bildung der Jugend", in *Bildung und Entfaltung der Individualität*, p. 57.
[19] Jn 3:30.

last end is unattainable."[20] Christ Himself established the community of the Church for our salvation, and thus it is clear that God wills for us to be in community. In a beautiful way, Edith Stein asserts that man "is born from community, in community, and for community".[21] Born from the communion of husband and wife, into the community of the family, every human person is born for the community of heaven.

Given our fallen human nature, we come into the world as selfish creatures, concerned only about "me". To live in community, we must instead begin to think of "us". The role of the school is to help students to become members of communities.

On the first day of school, there is no community between the students and the teacher. The teacher who sees this role as one of service, not domination, will have an attitude of love and reverence toward the children from the start. These attitudes provide the atmosphere in which community can develop. When the child knows that he is loved, says Edith Stein, "the child's heart easily opens up, and this provides the first insight into the uniqueness of the individual".[22] When the teacher has a love and reverence for the students, then "she *is* already in community with them even before the external community life begins".[23]

The study of various subjects in school is not only important in itself but is also helpful in forming a community. By

---

[20] Stein, "Die theoretischen Grundlagen der sozialen Bildungsarbeit", in *Bildung und Entfaltung der Individualität*, p. 16. Cf. ibid., p. 18: "*Community is necessary for salvation.*"

[21] Ibid., p. 18.

[22] Ibid., p. 32.

[23] Ibid.

means of their study of mathematics or science or reading, the children will begin to discern their place in the Mystical Body of Christ. Since the child's role in the Mystical Body of Christ will be to use his strengths for the good of all, the teacher ought to be attentive to recognizing each child's talents and weaknesses and to giving each child the opportunity to cultivate these strengths and to make them useful for the whole community. The child who is a good artist can help the teacher to make drawings on the board. The child who excels in mathematics may be able to help those who have difficulty with that subject.

In this way, children learn to give and to receive help. A community, a working together, then arises. Rather than competing against one another, students learn to help one another. In such an environment, every child experiences that he has talents and weaknesses. Each one can trust that others will help in difficulties, while each, in turn, can make his talents useful for all. Such an exchange is characteristic of community. As the child discovers his role in the community of the classroom—perhaps he is the expert artist or the leader during recess—he also begins to discover something about his vocation in life.

The role of the teacher as described by Edith Stein is a daunting one, yet to teachers she offers these words of encouragement:

> The educator should be convinced that his efforts are important, even though he cannot always measure the results of his efforts, even though sometimes he can never be aware

of them at all. He must never forget that, above all, the primary and most essential Educator is not the human being but God Himself. He gives nature as He does life's circumstances under which it comes to development; He also has the power to transform nature from within and to intervene with His works where human powers fail. If religious education succeeds in breaking down resistance to divine instruction, then one can be certain about everything else. We should also be convinced that, in the divine economy of salvation, no sincere effort remains fruitless even when human eyes can perceive nothing but failures.[24]

In their task of forming young people in the spirituality of communion, teachers are essential to the new evangelization. The community life children experience at school prepares them to become living members of the Body of Christ and to establish good Christian families, living in communion with Christ and His will.

[24] Stein, "Spirituality of the Christian Woman", in *Essays on Woman*, p. 107.

6

Communion of Heart and Soul

In his work *Being and Time*, Martin Heidegger makes the well-known assertion that we find ourselves "thrown into the world". This phrase evokes the image of our being violently cast into the world and being left there to fend for ourselves. Indeed, sometimes we do feel as though we have been thrown into the world. Our world can be a lonely, competitive, and hostile environment.

The image that contrasts most strikingly with that of being thrown into the world is that of "being at home". Thrown into the world, we are alone and isolated; at home, we are in the company of those we know and love. Thrown into the world, we struggle to survive or to succeed; at home, we are safe. Thrown into the world, we must fight; at home, we rejoice in being with those we love.

The word *home* reminds us of our family life, and, indeed, the family is the primary place where we are meant to be at home. It is not *only* with our families, however, that we can be at home: we can be at home with Christ and in our life with Him; we can be at home in the Church, with our friends, in our vocation, in our place of work. We can also experience in these situations the hostility and the isolation of being thrown into the world.

Each of us longs to be at home, and this desire is our God-given longing for our ultimate communion with Him in heaven. During our sojourn through this life, we will never be wholly at home; our true home is in heaven. Each of us lives in various communities—the family, the workplace, the classroom, the parish, the convent, the rectory—and, as a member of these communities, each of us is responsible for making these communities a home, and for meeting the challenge of making "the Church *the home and the school of communion*".[1]

Association versus Community

In the introduction to her treatise on community, "Individual and Community", Edith Stein makes an important distinction: "Under 'community' is understood the natural, organic union of individuals; under 'association' is understood a union that is rational and mechanical."[2] A community arises naturally like an organism; an association is created like a

---

[1] John Paul II, Apostolic Letter *Novo Millennio Ineunte* (Boston: Pauline Books and Media, 2001), no. 43.

[2] Edith Stein, "Individual and Community", in *The Collected Works of Edith Stein*, vol. 7, *Philosophy of Psychology and the Humanities*, trans. Sister Mary Catharine Baseheart, S.C.N., and Marianne Sawicki, ed. Marianne Sawicki (Washington, D.C.: ICS Publications, 2000), p. 130.

machine.[3] In an association "one person approaches another as *subject* to *object*", whereas in community one lives with another "*as a subject* and does not confront him but rather *lives with him* ... forming a *community*".[4]

To explain further the distinction between the two realities, Edith Stein uses the example of a demagogue, who studies the people so that he can make them subservient to his own purposes.[5] In an association, one looks *at* others as objects; in community, one is bound *with* them as a subject to other subjects. Although Edith uses a negative example to explain the nature of an association, an association, as such, is not a negative reality. An association is negative when one lives exclusively in the associational stance (i.e., always approaching persons as objects rather than as subjects).

An association is defined by its goal, and to accomplish its goal, it has determined functions. In a factory, for instance, the goal of manufacturing a given product is attained through the cooperation of people who serve in various functions: some functions are manual, others managerial or secretarial. An individual who joins the association of the factory takes his place in one such preexisting function. If he cannot fulfill one of these functions, he cannot join the association; he cannot work at the factory. If no individual can fill a given function, then the function (or office) remains empty. If too many functions remain empty—if there is no one to serve as

[3] See ibid., pp. 261–62.
[4] Ibid., p. 130.
[5] See ibid., p. 131.

manager of the factory, for example—then the association of the factory ceases to exist.[6]

Edith Stein explains that community is organic, that it develops and grows naturally, unlike an association. We see this most clearly in the community of a family, in which the marital life and the love of a man and a woman naturally lead to a growth in the community through the birth of children. In her work *Finite and Eternal Being*, Sister Teresa Benedicta uses the community of the Church to explain the organic nature of community. Saint Paul describes the Church as the Body of Christ, and as such she is not "an arbitrarily and artificially constructed institutional 'mechanism,' but a living or organic whole".[7] Although some mistakenly view the Church as an association—consisting of artificial institutions and laws—she is, in fact, a community composed of human persons, with Christ as her Head.[8]

The "We" of Community

As she did in her dissertation on empathy, Edith Stein provides an experiential example to explain further the nature of community: "Suppose we take the following as an example. The army unit in which I'm serving is grieving over the loss

[6] See ibid., pp. 255ff.

[7] *The Collected Works of Edith Stein*, vol. 9, *Finite and Eternal Being*, trans. Kurt F. Reinhardt, ed. L. Gelber and R. Leuven, O.C.D. (Washington, D.C.: ICS Publications, 2002), p. 413.

[8] See Stein, *Finite and Eternal Being*, pp. 412–13, for a beautiful exposition on the life of the community of the Church.

of its leader."[9] In this grief, which is experienced together, we experience belonging to a common "we". Edith is quick to point out that this "we" has its source in the individual persons, of course, since there is no separate subsisting "we". There is a certain grief that a person feels as a member of the community, although there can also be some aspect of personal grief, not common to all, that one feels in addition to the grief felt as part of the "we".[10] If the individual did not belong to the unit, he would not be grieving the loss of his leader.[11]

One can certainly say that a community has feelings and experiences, as the example above shows. "It makes perfect sense to say that the community is grieving deeply, passionately, and persistently; or, mildly and fleetingly",[12] even though the community is not a superindividual and has no consciousness, as an individual person does.[13]

What kind of experiences can be part of such a communal experience? In her dissertation on empathy, Edith Stein explains that the human person has several levels: the physical, the psychic, the spiritual (by which she does not mean "religious", but something like "mental"), and the soul. The physical level includes all the purely physical experiences and feelings. The psychic level is closely related to the physical

[9] Stein, "Individual and Community", in *Philosophy of Psychology and the Humanities*, p. 134.

[10] See ibid., p. 136.

[11] One who does not belong to the unit can grieve the loss of the person, but it would be an experientially distinct experience.

[12] Stein, "Individual and Community", in *Philosophy of Psychology and the Humanities*, p. 139.

[13] See ibid., pp. 139–40.

level and depends upon it and includes our energy (both mental and bodily) and our moods. The spiritual level is the level of rationality, and it includes thinking, motivation, perception of the good, and willing. Edith says that the last level, the soul, is our "core" and our uniqueness.

The levels of our psychic and spiritual being are shareable, and on the basis of shared thoughts, motives, and feelings, the experience of "we" can arise. The things that happen on the purely physical level and those that happen in our soul are in principle unshareable. No one else can have a direct experience of my physical sensations, and no human person can reach into the depths of my soul. Without doubt, one can empathize with another who has cold feet, but one cannot *actually* share the sensation.[14]

Since not all aspects of the individual person can be held in common, community is necessarily limited. In addition to this necessary limitation, our fallen nature and our actual sinfulness also limit community. Our inclinations to selfishness and our lack of generosity limit what we contribute to community. In the community of the saints and the angels, the limitation caused by sinfulness is not present.

The Good of Community

Edith Stein suggests, but does not develop, that living in community is a good as such and that the common life itself is the

---

[14] See ibid., pp. 145ff.

end and focus of the community.[15] Speaking of education, she says: "When a human person has become a living member of the Church and when his entire life is determined and ordered to this membership, then, in the Catholic sense, he has been formed and his arrival at the final goal is as sure as it can be in *statu viae*."[16] The goal of the formation of the human person is membership in the community of the Mystical Body. Membership in the community of the Church is the end and is a good in itself. It seems true that community is a good as such and requires no further end to justify its existence or its goodness. In fact, life in communion is the deepest vocation of the Church and of each member of the Church.[17]

As wayfarers on this earth, we are always *becoming*, so that neither we nor the communities to which we belong are complete or perfect.[18] Communities on this earth are always a school, and it is through life in community that human persons are able to develop and to become what they are meant to be as individuals. It seems, therefore, that a community of human persons on earth serves the members, since the

[15] See ibid., p. 251: "Also, it doesn't serve any external purpose, like an association, but rather—like an organism—has no other purpose than that immanent to it, the purpose of proper development, of the unfolding of its original predisposition."

[16] Edith Stein, "Jugendbildung im Licht des katholischen Glaubens", in *Edith Stein Gesamtausgabe*, vol. 16, *Bildung und Entfaltung der Individualität: Beiträge zum christlichen Erziehungsauftrag*, ed. Sister Maria Amata Neyer, O.C.D., and Beate Beckmann-Zöller (Freiburg im Breisgau: Herder, 2001), pp. 87–88.

[17] See *Catechism of the Catholic Church*, 2nd ed. (Washington, D.C.: Libreria Editrice Vaticana, 2000), no. 959, s.v. "communion".

[18] See Stein, "Die theoretischen Grundlagen der sozialen Bildungsarbeit", in *Bildung und Entfaltung der Individualität*, p. 20.

community has no life apart from the members. The good attained in community is the good of the members, the highest good being the eternal salvation of each.[19]

Among the communities Edith Stein mentions as examples are the army unit, the nation, and the classroom. All these communities have for their purpose not only or primarily the good of their members, but also some other good. Insofar as these communities have a goal, are they then like an association? It seems not. The goals of an association are determinate and finite. The goods that unite members in community are eternal goods or ideals, goods that one never obtains in full. The protection of the people, which is the goal of the army unit, and the attainment of knowledge, which is the goal of school, are goals that one never attains in a definitive manner. A community is more permanent than an association that has a finite goal.[20] The common goal or

[19] In the past, many religious congregations stated their express purpose to be "the glory of God and the sanctification of the members". Then, having stated the main purpose, they specified how God was to be glorified and the members to be sanctified through the specific apostolic works or charisms. See *Guide to the Catholic Sisterhoods in the United States*, compiled by Thomas P. McCarthy, C.S.V. (Washington, D.C.: The Catholic University of America Press, 1955), for many examples of the purpose of various religious institutes in the United States prior to the Second Vatican Ecumenical Council. Since the Second Vatican Council, religious institutes do not typically refer to the "purpose" of the institute but to its *charism*.

[20] See Stein, "Individual and Community", in *Philosophy of Psychology and the Humanities*, p. 272: "But community will posses that much higher of a value for the individuals the more deeply they root themselves in it. This connection is clear with communities that ground themselves in positive convictions". It is possible that the acts of perceiving others, appraising others, and so forth can lead to an associational attitude, but it can "also become the basis for new

objective can also be called a common vision, even if Edith Stein does not use that terminology. She mentions, too, that communities such as friendship and marriage arise on the basis of shared convictions.[21]

There is a wide variety of communities, some of which arise in a natural fashion from people who happen to find themselves together, as can happen in a classroom, while others arise almost like an association, insofar as members choose to become members when they wish to share in the common vision, as in the case of a person entering a religious institute. There are also some communities into which one is simply born, and one may or may not have the sense of belonging to it, even though one does in fact depend on it, as may be the case in the community of a nation.[22]

Some communities bind us deeply to other members; others affect us more superficially. The community of the family

---

modes of communal living [other] than those considered up till now, those of communal direction toward an object: modes that are of an entirely separate significance for the evolution of that which we are calling a genuine community" (ibid., p. 266). "We saw the essence of communal life directly in the fact that the subjects aren't directed at one another but are communally turned toward an objective" (ibid., p. 270).

[21] See ibid., p. 284: "Friendship and marriage are communities that grow up on grounds of unifying convictions."

[22] See ibid., p. 281: With regard to persons who belong to the community but do not live as members, Edith Stein says that "this doesn't happen with communities that have grown up on grounds of positive convictions of the individuals forming them (with a friendship or marriage), but it might happen with those that develop solely on the basis of a common life. In a nation there could be living countless [persons] who bear its stamp but don't feel like they belong to it and don't co-experience its fates."

or of the Church affects many aspects of our lives and therefore binds us more deeply to the other members than does our membership in a nation. The more deeply a community affects the individuals and the more the members devote themselves to the life of the community, the stronger the community will be.[23]

Edith Stein notes that there must be communal aspects in every association and that a community, too, oftentimes has admixtures of association.[24] A community may undertake some project, for example, and, to that end, assign members to perform various tasks, as in an association. In organizing the project, one of the members of the community must take an "associational stance" in looking *at* the members and judging who would best be able to fulfill a given task, for instance.

In community, members are bound by a common vision, and it is therefore indispensable that they be of one mind and soul with respect to the common vision. There is a unity in community. Disagreement about the common vision is destructive to the community, and its result can be that the community "splits up and breaks apart into a plurality of communities (I'm thinking of something like the splitting of parties or religious communities)".[25] It is also important to realize that in community we need not share *all* of our motives and ideas in common. There may be legitimate

[23] See ibid., p. 272.
[24] See ibid., pp. 130–31.
[25] Ibid., p. 281.

diversity in any community about those issues that do not pertain to the common vision.

It is not sufficient for members of a community to have a common vision, but they must also tend toward this vision *together*. It is possible for each to have the same vision and to tend toward it individually, but there would then be no community. In the thinking together that is characteristic of a community, one member not only understands the other but also *adopts* the other's way of thinking. Edith Stein says that in this "'exchange of thoughts' a thinking-together arises that no longer is experienced as an experience of one or the other, but as *our* common thinking".[26] Edith Stein once again uses an example to clarify her meaning. Suppose, she says, that she has the desire to see her friends. By means of a messenger, she sends them an invitation to come for a visit. On the basis of this invitation, her friends may share her desire to meet. They will then be motivated to come at her invitation. Then she and her friends all share one motive: to meet with one another. This one motive inspires all to action: it motivates the friends to come for a visit, as it motivated the host to invite them.[27] "If a plurality of subjects is filled with *one* objective, then what results is *one* community-wide stance of will and *one* action, no matter whether everybody's doing 'the same thing' or whether they're carrying out different component actions towards the realization of the collective goal."[28]

[26] Ibid., p. 170.
[27] See ibid., p. 192.
[28] Ibid., p. 193.

Communal Energy and Character

Edith Stein says that there is such a thing as communal energy.[29] The community's energy has not only quantity but also quality. Taking an associational stance (of looking at a community as an object, instead of living in it as a subject), one observes that some communities are joyful, some seem sluggish, some are agitated, et cetera. Some communities seem to have great physical energy, while others excel in intellectual energy and make important contributions to the intellectual world.

How does the communal energy come into being? Whenever a member lives *as a member*, he contributes to the communal energy. Whenever he acts not as a member but *as* and *for himself*, he does not contribute to the communal energy. One can even abuse the communal energy for selfish ends.[30] Edith Stein says that, typically, individuals do not contribute *all* their energy to a single community, but "each one retains certain 'reserves' for his or her individual living."[31]

---

[29] The word Edith Stein uses for this energy is *lebenskraft*, literally "lifepower". Although *lifepower* is more accurate, it sounds strange to those who speak English, even conjuring up images of the movie *Star Wars*, and so I have rendered the term as "energy". Sister Mary Catharine Baseheart, S.C.N., and Marianne Sawicki use the translation "lifepower". See ibid., pp. 200ff.

[30] See Stein, "Individual and Community", in *Philosophy of Psychology and the Humanities*, p. 204.

[31] Ibid., p. 203. See also ibid., p. 280. There are certain circumstances in which one cannot retain "reserves for individual living", although such a reservation is in other cases appropriate. During the First World War, Edith Stein saw it as her duty to spend herself wholly for the good of her country. See *The Collected Works of Edith Stein*, vol. 1, *Life in a Jewish Family (1891–1916)*,

Not only does the member reserve some energy for himself, but each member also belongs to a range of communities and distributes his energy among them, in varying degrees. A community embracing more aspects of one's life calls for a greater contribution of energy. The nation affects only the most public aspects of an individual's life, and therefore an individual usually contributes only a small amount of his energy to the community of the nation. An individual's family embraces a much larger aspect of his life and calls for a greater contribution of energy. An individual can contribute various kinds of energy—some give more psychophysical energy, others intellectual energy, and still others mediate the energy of grace.

In any community, some individuals contribute much while others contribute little. Individuals also contribute different proportions of their energy. Someone with much energy can assist the community more by contributing a small share of his energy than an individual with little energy can aid by contributing all his energy. Given the relationship of individual to communal energy, it follows that "the power of a community can be increased in two ways: by receiving new powerful individuals, and by demanding more from those who already belong to it. Accordingly, it can be weakened in two ways: if its components drift off, and if

trans. Sister Josephine Koeppel, O.C.D., ed. L. Gelber and R. Leuven, O.C.D. (Washington, D.C.: ICS Publications, 1986), p. 297: "'I have no private life anymore,' I told myself. 'All my energy must be devoted to this great happening. Only when the war is over, if I'm alive then, will I be permitted to think of my private affairs once more.'"

the individuals belonging to it slacken in their accomplishments for the community."[32]

A community's character is closely related to its energy. *Character*, in regard to an individual person, refers to his moral qualities, which are developed by his free choices. Community has a character only in an analogical sense, again, because it is not a substance but is a reality that arises on the basis of interrelationships among persons. In ordinary language, we attribute character to a community. We speak of communities such as nations, families, and religious institutes as having the characteristics of being hospitable, intellectual, generous, artistic, et cetera. A community depends for its character, as it does for all things, upon its members. A member contributes to building the communal character when he responds to a good *as* a member (not as an individual).[33]

An example will make this a little clearer. A man may be very generous in giving of himself to his family. Since he is generous as a *father and a husband*, he gives the community of his family a certain generous character. But when it comes to his nation, this same man may lack generosity. He gives neither his time nor his energy nor his thought to the nation. Since he does not live generously as a *member of his nation*, the man's generosity does not make the nation more generous. Clearly, those people who do not live as *members*, who live physically in a community, but who neither think nor act as members, do not contribute to its character.

---

[32] See Stein, "Individual and Community", in *Philosophy of Psychology and the Humanities*, p. 206.

[33] The level at which a community affects an individual also determines the extent to which the community will have a distinct character.

The Importance of Attitudes

Typically, we live within a community and sometimes also confront it as an object. Enjoying an event as part of the family, we are immersed in the community. Even while we partake of this event, an attitude of gratitude for the community may arise in us, and this attitude indicates that we are focusing on the community as an objective whole. According to Edith Stein, our living within community and with its members is the original and most natural stance. She says that in our everyday life we are for the most part " 'oriented' to individual persons.... Indeed, we see the lone [community member] *along with* what accrues to him or her 'because of the community,' but we don't see the community that's standing behind him or her."[34] At the same time, though, it "pertains to the essence of the social whole that the single members don't just live as members, but can confront it and make it into an object". Edith Stein then continues: "For example, I don't just live as a citizen; I can contemplate my nation and my state. I love them and make sacrifices for them."[35]

Edith Stein explains that the attitude that the members bear toward the communities to which they belong is key for the community's life. She uses the example of our attitude toward our country. Although we do not love or know individually every member of our country, we can have a love for the country as a whole, and such an attitude is

[34] Stein, "Individual and Community", in *Philosophy of Psychology and the Humanities*, p. 196.
[35] Ibid., p. 215.

important because it motivates acts of service. When members love their community, they will be motivated to act for its good. In addition to motivating actions, an individual's attitude toward the community also affects other members (for good or for ill). Edith Stein provides the following example: "The love that I harbor for my nation deploys its efficacy for the nation first of all within me, for the love enhances my powers and impels me to devote them more intensely to the nation's service and to live in a greater measure as its member. Furthermore, the love can carry others away as well, that is, inspire patriotism in them too, and thereby increase their powers and supply those enhanced powers to the community."[36] Moreover, the love that we bear for our country can enable others to feel loved "in the name of the community"[37] and be strengthened by that. Our attitude toward the community is essential, therefore, to its well-being.

In chapter 2, it was mentioned that openness toward another person is indispensable for empathy. In community, too, members cannot unite with one another, cannot form a bond, unless they are receptive to one another. "Where the individuals are 'open' to one another ... there a communal life *subsists*, there the two are members of one whole; and *without* such a reciprocal relationship community isn't possible."[38] In this context, the associational attitude that sees

[36] Ibid.
[37] Ibid.
[38] Ibid., p. 214.

the other as an object is toxic to the life of the community.[39] Motivations cannot interweave when one person views another as an object. Edith Stein emphasizes: "Instead of monadic closure, community demands open and naïve commitment: not separated but common living, fed from common sources and stirred by common motives."[40] In *Finite and Eternal Being*, Sister Teresa Benedicta of the Cross highlights again the importance of the attitude of openness, of receptiveness to the other:

> Human souls are capable, by virtue of their free spirituality, of opening themselves in loving self-giving to one another and of receiving one another into their own selves—never, to be sure, as completely as is the case with a soul that abides in God, but in some greater or smaller measure. And this receiving is not merely a knowing comprehension which leaves the *object* [*Gegenstand*] standing by itself at a distance and is thus of small significance for the soul, but an inward reception of the object, a reception which aids in nourishing and forming the soul.[41]

The attitude of viewing the community as an object *is* necessary, for example, for the leader who must guide it or for a member in order to have affection for the whole, but one needs always to return to the simple living in community and not remain in the attitude of the outsider.

[39] See ibid.
[40] Ibid., p. 215.
[41] Stein, *Finite and Eternal Being*, p. 514.

Communal Carriers

To the extent that an individual lives *as* a member, to the extent that he lives in the communal "we", to the extent that he is directed toward the communal vision and shares the communal motives, he is what Edith Stein calls a carrier of the communal life (*Träger des Gemeinschaftslebens*). As a carrier, he is a living member of the community, has a communal consciousness, and identifies his good with the good of the community.

The carriers form the "core" of the community; they shape its character and guarantee its existence. Edith Stein clarifies that "the more carriers a community has to support it, and the further their devotion to it extends, the more secure its substance and the more assured its outward demeanor."[42] The carriers set the tone in the community. It is largely the carriers, therefore, who determine whether a community will be a "home". The life of the community both depends upon its carriers and becomes visible in them. Sometimes a single strong carrier can give a community its character and can unite it, but, "if he alone is the soul of the whole, then it falls apart with his departure."[43] Those who have positions of leadership in a community—the teacher in a classroom or the leaders of an army unit, for example—should be carriers of the community, but such is not always the case. Any member of the community can, in principle, be a carrier.

[42] Stein, "Individual and Community", in *Philosophy of Psychology and the Humanities*, p. 281.

[43] Ibid. Translation altered by Sister M. Regina van den Berg, F.S.G.M.

Not all the individuals who belong to the community need to be carriers, however.[44] In a nation, for example, there are many who experience the community solely as an environment, and they do not feel that they belong to it.[45] Those who are not carriers are not necessarily useless to the community, because "the community avails itself of their work and employs them in the total operation of its life, even though they themselves don't feel like members."[46] If *no* members were communal carriers, however, the community would fail to be a unified personality, and there would be only "an illusion of it without concord",[47] because the members would lack inner unity.

Even though the Holy See's Instruction *Fraternal Life in Community* is directed to members of institutes of the consecrated life, the distinction it makes between mere "consumers" of community and "builders" of community fits well with Edith Stein's notion of carriers and is applicable to life in community in general. The Instruction underlines the importance of forming members to be builders, not merely consumers:

> If it is true that communion does not exist without the self-offering of each member, then it is necessary, right from the beginning, to remove the illusion that everything must come from others, and to help each one discover with gratitude all that has already been received, and is in fact being received

[44] See ibid., p. 280.
[45] See ibid., p. 281.
[46] Ibid.
[47] Ibid.

from others. Right from the beginning, it is necessary to prepare them to be not only consumers of community, but above
all its builders; to be responsible for each other's growth; to
be open and available to receive the gift of the other; to be
able to help and to be helped; to replace and to be replaced.[48]

Individuality in Community

Even though community arises on the basis of shareable and
shared content, the unshareable personal level is relevant to
the individual's life in community. Also, an individual's talents or abilities, even when they are not what binds him in
community, can be useful in community. The distinctiveness of each person prescribes his particular role within community. The community's "predisposition is based in the
distinctiveness of the individuals who enter into the community, [and] so are all organs and functionings that build up the
community determined in the same way."[49]

The role of the individual within community can be clar-
ified by contrasting it to his role in an association. An association, as was already mentioned, is defined by its goal, and
to accomplish its goal an association has determined functions. The one who becomes part of the association must

[48] Congregation for Institutes of Consecrated Life and Societies of Apostolic
Life, *Fraternal Life in Community* (Vatican City State: Libreria Editrice Vaticana,
1994), no. 24.

[49] Stein, "Individual and Community", in *Philosophy of Psychology and the
Humanities*, p. 261.

find his place in one of the predetermined functions. If the individual cannot fulfill one of the preexisting functions, he cannot join the association. In a community, the individuals who become members of the community *create* certain functions that correspond to their particular disposition. Edith Stein does not use the word *functions* to name these things, but calls them "organs" because they arise naturally within a community and are not artificially created. A member with artistic talent may put this talent to use for the community. Should this artist leave the community, the artistic aspect of the community may cease altogether. The particular individuals determine the direction of the community from within; it is not prescribed from without. Edith Stein compares the functions of an association to the organs of a community in this way: "Functional modes [in community] can't be 'created' but then fail to be suitably occupied afterwards (like 'offices' in an association), because organs are formed only insofar as the material necessary for them is available. This or that organ is replaceable; individuals can leave and new ones enter without the community's ceasing to exist. Perhaps it alters its character in such an exchange, certain organs die away (or functionings cease) and new ones form."[50]

A community is more flexible than an association. Since a community is not defined by a specific goal, it can develop and change. When a given organ ceases to exist, the community as such does not necessarily cease to exist. An association, which is defined by a determined goal, lacks such flexibility.

[50] Ibid.

Should certain of its functions cease, the association itself would cease to exist.

Each member's individuality is important for a community insofar as it determines his role within the community, as Edith Stein affirms:

> Individuality has a positive meaning for social life. A person's individuality indicates which position is appropriate for him in this or that smaller community, and perhaps indicates even his position in the entire development of humanity. Community is a body with diverse members, and the variety of individualities corresponds to the variety of functions within the larger body. Since one individual is suitable for this, and another is suitable for another function as a member, no arbitrary exchange of individuals, especially of members, is possible.[51]

The goal of formation is to help the individual to develop and harmonize the two aspects of his being: to unfold his individuality and to become a communal member.[52] Edith Stein writes that "the *task of social formation is necessary* because man does not come into the world as a finished community member, because membership and community must

---

[51] Stein, "Die theoretischen Grundlagen der sozialen Bildungsarbeit", in *Bildung und Entfaltung der Individualität*, p. 24.

[52] Guidance is needed especially for one's supernatural growth, says Edith Stein. See ibid., p. 17: "Only in very exceptional cases can a human person succeed in making his way to heaven all alone and relying only upon himself. Even most of those people who have left the world in order to dedicate themselves exclusively to working for the Kingdom of Heaven would be lost if they did not bind themselves to a community with an established Rule of life."

develop and, we can now add to this, because in the double nature of man—the individual and the member nature—
there are possibilities of conflict and dangers that can perhaps
be avoided by means of an appropriate formation."[53] Formation is needed in the development of the individual because
the danger is that the two aspects fail to harmonize: that one
individuality becomes so powerful that it excludes his life in
community or that the communal life suffocates his individuality. According to Edith Stein, the latter is the greater danger
for the majority of persons.[54]

Edith Stein observes that the individual and the community depend upon one another and develop together: "As a
new member grows into the community and unfolds himself as a member, the community itself undergoes a change
and development. In this way, community, membership, and
individuality grow and develop side-by-side and with one
another."[55] Individuality and community are inseparable:
neither can be isolated from the other. For this reason, Edith
warns that "he who wants to emphasize the importance of
the one at the cost of the other injures both, because community is founded on individuals as an organism arises from its

---

[53] Ibid., p. 20.

[54] See ibid., pp. 21–22: "For the majority of people there is more danger
that their individuality is choked in community than that the community is
destroyed by their individuality. Their 'own' is too weak to show itself and to
assert itself when it is confronted on all sides with what is other. The 'own' does
not dare to assert itself and it must therefore atrophy. This cannot be considered a happy development, neither for the individual nor for the community,
which, after all, depends upon the strengths of individuals."

[55] Ibid., p. 20.

many varied members. He who injures one member harms
the entire organism. Separated from the organism no member can exist."[56]

The Angelic Community

Rational creatures are images of God in a particular way,
so that "every communion and community of finite persons has its primordial paradigm [*Urbild*] in the Divine Trinity, although the image ... is infinitely far removed from
the *Urbild* and very imperfect."[57] Sister Teresa Benedicta
of the Cross concludes a section of *Finite and Eternal Being*
that examines the difference between the image of God in
rational creatures and the rest of creation by remarking that
"both a genuine natural communal life and the life of grace
and glory presuppose personal self-giving and are therefore
special character marks by which created spirits—angels and
human beings—excel all other things and beings in the created universe."[58]

No angel lives as a "self-enclosed world apart from the
others",[59] but each is united to the others in a communal
life that Sister Teresa Benedicta likens to the structure of a
well-ordered state.[60] Insofar as human communities rest on

[56] Ibid., p. 23.
[57] Stein, *Finite and Eternal Being*, p. 466.
[58] Ibid.
[59] Ibid., p. 411.
[60] See ibid., p. 412.

a spiritual foundation, the angelic community "is the ideal archetype of all human community and social order".[61]

The energy that flows through the angelic community comes from "the divine head as the source from which flows the life of grace".[62] The angels are open to receiving grace from God, and they are "also open to each other, so that the higher ones are capable of communicating their spiritual life to the lower ones, and the lower ones are capable of receiving the gifts of the higher ones".[63]

The interaction between the higher and lower angels is perfectly ordered, and each angel occupies that position for which he is by nature suited; "each member spirit stands in its proper place and desires no other."[64] Among the angels, "there is neither false assertion nor a withholding, for the sake of *self-aggrandizement*, of the received fullness of grace, nor a presumptuous self-sufficiency that closes itself to the influx of the abundance of grace."[65] The higher angels share with the lower ones without envy, and if they keep something back, they do so for the good of the weaker spirit.[66]

The angelic community is an archetype and model for human communities in which individuals often fail to occupy that place in community for which their individuality suits them, as Edith Stein had noted elsewhere. Like

[61] Ibid.
[62] Ibid., p. 414.
[63] Ibid.
[64] Ibid., p. 416.
[65] Ibid., pp. 415–16.
[66] See ibid., p. 416.

the angels, the human person is *free*, and once he attains the use of his freedom, "he is no longer simply handed over to the community, but he can give himself to the community or close himself to it; he can accept this or that role in it or he can refuse it."[67] Unlike the community of the angels, wherein each takes the place that his individuality prescribes for him, Edith Stein observes, even when individual persons know themselves and know the role that is fitting for them in community, they still "constantly strive after offices and positions for which they are by nature in no way suited ... [so that] the most different applicants vie for the same place".[68] Unlike the angels, "man flees from himself in illusions and self-deceptions because he does not *want* to see the truth that contradicts his wishes."[69]

The Mystical Body

Sister Teresa Benedicta concludes her final philosophical work, *Finite and Eternal Being*, with a study of the community of the Mystical Body of Christ. In her usual manner, she turns to something that is closer to our experience, in this case, our membership in the community of mankind. Each individual belongs as a member to mankind. We experience being a member of mankind as a fact, even though

---

[67] Stein, "Die theoretischen Grundlagen der sozialen Bildungsarbeit", in *Bildung und Entfaltung der Individualität*, pp. 24–25.

[68] Ibid., p. 25.

[69] Ibid.

this realization requires a level of maturity. Early in life we begin by recognizing the community of the family. We are not yet aware of larger communities such as our people, the state, or even less the whole of mankind. Moreover, we often grasp the unity of our smaller communities by viewing them in contrast to other communities, and in this way we experience these other communities as foreign. It is important to experience the community of the whole of mankind, notes Sister Teresa Benedicta, because when we do this, we do not stand in contrast to any other, and then no one is foreign to us. Being members of mankind, it "is of signal importance for us to realize experientially that common bond which links us—notwithstanding all the differences—with people and individuals of every age and clime, and to be conscious of the fact that by our own contact with foreign members of the human race our own being is enriched and perfected".[70]

Mankind is the essential foundation for the community of the Mystical Body because Christ became man: "Humankind is the portal through which the Word of God entered into the created world."[71] Salvation history is the history of the whole of mankind in union with the *one* God-man, the Head, in the one Mystical Body of Christ. Were it not for the presupposition that all mankind is one, and that man belongs by nature to the community of mankind, then Original Sin, whereby in one man all have sinned, would be entirely unintelligible.

[70] Stein, *Finite and Eternal Being*, p. 510.
[71] Ibid., p. 527.

Adam acted as a *member* and as *head* of mankind; therefore, his act affects all the members.[72]

Were all mankind not one, it would be equally unintelligible how one man's act could save all. Christ, acting as God and as a member of mankind, by His redeeming act can affect all the members of mankind. His divinity *can* expiate, and His human nature makes it possible for Him both to suffer and to die *as* a member of mankind and *for* this community. One member can act on behalf of all; therefore, Christ can act to expiate for all members. Christ can act only for those who are in communion with Him, and when an individual is in communion with Christ, "then God is prone to see in Christ any repentant sinner and to accept Christ's atonement for all sins".[73]

In principle, the community of the Mystical Body of Christ extends as far as the community of mankind, and one ordinarily becomes a member through baptism. "Every individual human being is created to be a member of this [Mystical] body."[74] As a spiritual reality, the Mystical Body of Christ receives its energy wholly from Christ, and the members, insofar as they are members, participate in this energy of grace: "The life of grace flows into the members because *by their very nature* they are related to the head and—as spiritual beings and by virtue of their free openness—capable of receiving into themselves his divine life."[75] All the forms

---

[72] See above, p. 35, footnote 23.
[73] Stein, *Finite and Eternal Being*, p. 522.
[74] Ibid., p. 526.
[75] Ibid., p. 523.

of communion we experience during our earthly life are a preparation and a foretaste of the life of communion in heaven, our eternal goal and the apex of all communion. Each man becomes most fully of one heart and one soul with all the members of the Mystical Body of Christ in the fullness of eternal life. In one of her lectures on the vocation of man and woman, Edith Stein provides a succinct and attractive sketch of our life in communion, which serves well to conclude the present study:

> Christ is our head and His divine life overflows to us, His members, if we adhere to Him in love and we are subject to Him in obedience. The head is God Incarnate who has His autonomous existence beyond His Mystical Body. The members have their individual being as free and rational creatures, and the Mystical Body springs from the love of the head and a willing subordination of the members. The functions, which proceed from each member of the Mystical Body, are assigned to the member on the basis of the gifts of each, gifts of love and of spirituality; it is the wisdom of the head to utilize the members according to their gifts; but it is the divine power of the head to provide each individual member with gifts which can be of benefit to the entire organism. And it is the purpose of this entire body, the Mystical Body of Christ, that each individual member—who is indeed a whole human being with body and soul—attain to the fullness of salvation and sonship with God, and glorify in his own way the entire body, the communion of saints.[76]

[76] Stein, "Vocations of Man and Woman", in *The Collected Works of Edith Stein*, vol. 2, *Essays on Woman*, p. 68.

APPENDIX

The Examples of Our Lady and Saint Joseph

Our Lady and Saint Joseph provide us with witnesses of the meaning of true womanhood and true manhood.

We do not know much about Saint Joseph. One of the few things we are told about him is that he was a carpenter. As a man, who has a natural interest in work, it is fitting that Saint Joseph is identified according to his occupation. Saint Joseph, when already betrothed to our Lady, learned of her pregnancy and, with a heavy heart, decided to divorce her quietly. An angel came to him in a dream and told him: "Joseph, son of David, do not fear to take Mary your wife, for that which is conceived in her is of the Holy Spirit; she will bear a son, and you shall call his name Jesus, for he will save his people from their sins."[1] Upon receiving the angelic message, Saint Joseph did not fall into the typical masculine fault of seeking to know and understand fully even those things beyond our power to know and understand. Rather, he yielded, without recorded objection, to the angel's direction. Saint Joseph

[1] Mt 1:20–21.

models for all men docility to God. Men may be tempted to dominate, to control, to want to understand rationally. He shows men how to obey in faith.

After the birth of our Lord, the angel visited Saint Joseph again in a dream and commanded him: "Rise, take the child and his mother, and flee to Egypt, and remain there till I tell you."[2] Obedient to the angel, he "rose and took the child and his mother by night, and departed to Egypt".[3] It is interesting that the angel gives the warning not to our Lady, but to Saint Joseph. The angel appeared to him because it was his role to protect the Holy Family. It was at Saint Joseph's initiative, then, that the Holy Family fled to Egypt.

When Jesus was twelve years old, the Holy Family went on pilgrimage to Jerusalem. In Sacred Scripture we read: "[A]s they were returning, the boy Jesus stayed behind in Jerusalem. His parents did not know it."[4] After a day's journey, they noticed His absence and began to search among their kinsfolk and acquaintances. "After three days they found him in the temple, sitting among the teachers, listening to them and asking them questions."[5] Upon finding Jesus, Mary asked: "Son, why have you treated us so? Behold, your father and I have been looking for you anxiously."[6] In using the phrase "your father and I", our Lady points to Saint Joseph's role as father. As father, Saint Joseph guards the Child Jesus.

[2] Mt 2:13.
[3] Mt 2:14.
[4] Lk 2:43.
[5] Lk 2:46.
[6] Lk 2:48.

In the biological sense, Saint Joseph was not the father of Jesus, and his being called "father" initiates a new, spiritual fatherhood. It was to ensure fatherly protection for Jesus that God chose Joseph to be Mary's spouse.[7]

Saint Joseph's fatherhood is expressed concretely in his having made his life a service, a sacrifice to the Mystery of the Incarnation and to the redemptive mission connected with it; in having used his legal authority over the Holy Family in order to make a total gift of self, of his life and work; and in having turned his human vocation to domestic love into a superhuman oblation of self, an oblation of his heart and all his abilities into love placed at the service of the Messiah growing up in his house.[8]

At the Annunciation, our Lady conceives by the power of the Holy Spirit. She is therefore the model for both virgins and mothers. As Pope Saint John Paul II notes, "Motherhood implies from the beginning a special openness to the new person: and this is precisely the woman's part."[9] Our

[7] John Paul II, Apostolic Exhortation *Redemptoris Custos* (Vatican City State: Libreria Editrice Vaticana, 1989), no. 7: "In this family, Joseph is the father: his fatherhood is not one that derives from begetting offspring; but neither is it an 'apparent' or merely 'substitute' fatherhood. Rather, it is one that fully shares in authentic human fatherhood and the mission of a father in the family."

[8] See Paul VI, Homily for the Episcopal Consecration of Four Prelates of the Roman Curia (March 19, 1966): *Insegnamenti* IV (1966), p. 110, quoted in *Redemptoris Custos*, no. 8.

[9] John Paul II, Apostolic Letter *Mulieris Dignitatem*, "On the Dignity and Vocation of Women" (Vatican City State: Libreria Editrice Vaticana, 1988), no. 18.

Lady's words, "Let it be to me according to your word",[10] indicate her readiness to accept new life. Carrying the Christ Child in her womb, our Lady has an incomparable communion with Him. Edith Stein reflects: "She awaits His birth in blissful expectation; she watches over His childhood; near or far, indeed, wherever He wishes, she follows Him on His way."[11] In receiving the Christ Child, she does not receive Him as her own, as property, but "she has welcomed Him from God's hands; she lays Him back into God's hands by dedicating Him in the Temple and by being with Him at the crucifixion."[12]

The Blessed Mother at the wedding of Cana is a model for women, because she, true to her feminine nature, is attentive to the details of the wedding and, as Edith Stein notes, "in her quiet, observing look surveys everything and discovers what is lacking".[13] Even before others have noticed, before they can be embarrassed, "she has procured already the remedy."[14] She does not draw attention to herself, but points the stewards to her Son, and then leaves all in His hands. Edith Stein concludes: "Let her be the prototype of woman in professional life. Wherever situated, let her always perform her work quietly and dutifully, without claiming

[10] Lk 1:38.
[11] Edith Stein, "The Ethos of Women's Professions", in *The Collected Works of Edith Stein*, vol. 2, *Essays on Woman*, trans. Freda Mary Oben, ed. L. Gelber and R. Leuven, O.C.D., 2nd rev. ed. (Washington, D.C.: ICS Publications, 1996), p. 47.
[12] Ibid., p. 47.
[13] Ibid., p. 51.
[14] Ibid.

attention and appreciation. And at the same time, she should survey the conditions with a vigilant eye. Let her be conscious of where there is a want and where help is needed, intervening and regulating as far as it is possible in her power in a discreet way."[15]

[15] Ibid.

CHRONOLOGY OF SAINT TERESA BENEDICTA OF THE CROSS

October 12, 1891	Birth at Breslau, Germany (now Wrocław, Poland), on the Jewish Day of Atonement, as the youngest of seven (living) siblings.
July 10, 1893	Death of Siegfried Stein, Edith's father, of sunstroke.
October 12, 1897	Matriculation at Viktoria School in Breslau on her sixth birthday.
Easter 1906	Completion of Viktoria School and beginning of some months with her married sister Else.
Easter 1908	Successful completion of the examination for attendance at the *Oberlyceum* affiliated with Viktoria School.
1911	Successful completion of the *abitur* (comprehensive final examination), with distinction.
1911–1913	Studies at the University of Breslau (German studies, history, psychology, and philosophy).
1913–1915	Studies at the University of Göttingen (philosophy, German studies, history).
January 1915	Successful completion of the state doctoral examination at Göttingen, summa cum laude.

1915	Volunteer as a Red Cross nurse at a military hospital at Mährisch-Weisskirchen during World War I.
August 3, 1916	Successful completion of the doctoral examination at Freiburg, summa cum laude.
1916–1918	Assistant to Dr. Edmund Husserl at the University of Freiburg.
1917	Publication of her doctoral dissertation: *On the Problem of Empathy (Zum Problem der Einfühlung)*.
1919	Composition of "Psychic Causality" ("*Psychische Kausalität*") and "Individual and Community" ("*Individuum und Gemeinschaft*"), two treatises intended to obtain habilitation to teach at the university; published in 1922 in the *Jahrbuch für Philosophie und phänomenologische Forschung*.
Summer 1921	Reading of the *Life* of Saint Teresa of Jesus at the home of Theodor and Hedwig Conrad-Martius.
January 1, 1922	Baptism and First Communion by Dean Eugen Breitling at Saint Martin Parish in Bergzabern, taking the baptismal name of Theresia Hedwig.
February 2, 1922	Confirmation by Bishop Ludwig Sebastian, bishop of Speyer, in his private chapel.
Easter 1923– Easter 1931	Teacher at the Dominican Saint Magdalene teachers' training college, Speyer.
	Lecturer throughout Europe on pedagogy and the nature and the vocation of woman.

August 29, 1929	"The Role of the Educational Institutes of Religious in the Religious Formation of Youth" (*"Die Mitwirkung der klöster-lichen Bildungsanstalten an der religiösen Bildung der Jugend"*): probably a lecture given at an association of religious working in the apostolate of the education of young people.
April 24, 1930	"The Theoretical Foundations of Social Formation" (*"Die theoretischen Grundlagen der sozialen Bildungsarbeit"*): lecture given for the Bavarian Association of Catholic Teachers in Nuremberg.
July 14, 1930	"Eucharistic Formation" (*"Eucharistische Erziehung"*): lecture given at the Eucharistic Congress of German Speaking Countries in Speyer.
September 1, 1930	"The Ethos of Women's Professions" (*"Ethos der Frauenberufe"*): lecture given at the convention of the Association of Catholic Academics in Salzburg, Austria.
November 8, 1930	"Fundamental Principles of Women's Education" (*"Die Grundlagen der Frauenbildung"*): lecture given at the Education Committee of the Federation of German Catholic Women in Bendorf.
January 13, 1931	"The Mystery of Christmas: Incarnation and Humanity" (*"Das Weihnachtsgeheimnis: Menschwerdung und Menschheit"*): lecture given in Ludwigshafen.
March 26, 1931	Departure from Speyer.
October 30, 1931	"The Separate Vocations of Man and Woman according to Nature and Grace"

	(*"Beruf des Mannes und der Frau nach Natur- und Gnadenordnung"*): lecture given at the Academic Association at the Ursuline School in Aachen.
January 1932	"Spirituality of the Christian Woman" (*"Christliches Frauenleben"*): four lectures given at the Organization of Catholic Women in Zurich, Switzerland.
1932–1933	Lecturer at the German Institute for Scientific Pedagogy, Münster.
April 1, 1932	"The Art of Maternal Formation" (*"Mütterliche Erziehungskunst"*): radio lecture for Bavarian Radio in Munich.
April 23, 1932	"Problems of Women's Education" (*"Probleme der neueren Mädchenbildung"*): lecture given at the German Institute for Scientific Pedagogy.
January 5, 1933	"The Formation of Youth in Light of the Catholic Faith" (*"Jugendbildung im Licht des katholischen Glaubens"*): lecture given in the context of a course of the German Institute for Scientific Pedagogy in Berlin, Germany.
April 1933	Adolf Hitler's law forbidding Jews to hold teaching positions.
October 14, 1933	Entrance into the Cologne Carmel on the vigil of the feast of Saint Teresa of Jesus.
April 15, 1934	Investiture as a novice in the Cologne Carmel, taking the name Sister Teresa Benedicta of the Cross.
November 24, 1934?	"Love of the Cross: Some Thoughts for the Feast of Saint John of the Cross"

	("*Kreuzesliebe: Einige Gedanken zum Fest des hl. Vaters Johannes vom Kreuz*"): probably written shortly after her entrance into Carmel.
April 21, 1935	Profession of temporary vows (for three years) on Easter Sunday.
September 14, 1936	Death of her mother, Auguste Stein, on the feast of the Exaltation of the Holy Cross.
December 24, 1936	Baptism of her sister, Rosa Stein, in Cologne.
1937	Completion of *Finite and Eternal Being* (*Endliches und ewiges Sein*): published posthumously in 1950.
April 21, 1938	Profession of perpetual vows.
May 1, 1938	Reception of the black veil on Good Shepherd Sunday.
December 18, 1938	"How I Came to the Cologne Carmel" ("*Wie ich in der Kölner Karmel kam*"): essay prepared as a Christmas gift for her prioress, Mother Teresia Renata de Spiritu Sancto (Posselt).
December 31, 1938	Transfer from the Carmel in Cologne, Germany, to the Carmel in Echt, Netherlands.
1939	*Life in a Jewish Family (1891–1916)* (*Aus dem Leben einer Jüdischen Familie, Das Leben Edith Stein: Kindheit und Jugend*): the main part of the text was written in 1933.
September 12, 1939	"Elevation of the Cross, September 14, 1939: *Ave Crux, Spes Unica*"

	("*Kreuzerhöhung: Ave Cruz, Spes unica!*"): written for the community of sisters at Echt on the occasion of the annual renewal of vows on the feast of the Exaltation of the Cross on September 14.
1941	Work on *The Science of the Cross* (*Kreuzeswissenschaft*), in preparation for the fourth centenary of the birth of Saint John of the Cross, to be celebrated in 1942. The work was uncompleted.
July 26, 1942	Publication of a Pastoral Letter from the Dutch bishops, protesting the persecution of Jews in the Netherlands.
August 2, 1942	Retribution of the Nazis for the Pastoral Letter, with the arrest of a large number of Catholic Jews, including Sister Teresa Benedicta and her sister Rosa Stein.
August 9, 1942	Death of Sister Teresa Benedicta of the Cross and Rosa Stein in the gas chamber at Birkenau, Auschwitz.
May 1, 1987	Beatification as a martyr by Pope Saint John Paul II in Cologne, Germany.
October 11, 1998	Canonization by Pope Saint John Paul II in Rome.
October 1, 1999	Naming as copatroness of Europe along with Saint Bridget of Sweden and Saint Catherine of Siena.

BIBLIOGRAPHY

Benedict XVI. Encyclical Letter *Caritas in Veritate* [*Charity in Truth*]. Vatican City State: Libreria Editrice Vaticana, 2009.

Bouyer, Louis. *Dictionary of Theology*. Translated by Charles Underhill Quinn. New York: Desclee, 1965.

Catechism of the Catholic Church. 2nd ed. Washington, D.C.: United States Catholic Conference—Vatican City State: Libreria Editrice Vaticana, 2000.

Congregation for Institutes of Consecrated Life and Societies of Apostolic Life. *Fraternal Life in Community*. Vatican City State: Libreria Editrice Vaticana, 1994.

Graef, Hilda C. *The Scholar and the Cross: The Life and Work of Edith Stein*. Maryland: The Newman Press, 1955.

Hamans, Father Paul. *Edith Stein and Companions: On the Way to Auschwitz*. Translated by Sister M. Regina van den Berg, F.S.G.M. San Francisco: Ignatius Press, 2010.

Herbstrith, Waltraud. *Edith Stein: A Biography*. 2nd ed. Translated by Father Bernard Bonowitz, O.C.S.O. San Francisco: Ignatius Press, 1992.

John Paul II. Apostolic Letter *Mulieris Dignitatem* [*On the Dignity and Vocation of Women*]. Vatican City State: Libreria Editrice Vaticana, 1988.

———. Apostolic Letter *Novo Millennio Ineunte* [*At the Beginning of the New Millennium*]. Boston: Pauline Books and Media, 2001.

———. *The Original Unity of Man and Woman*. Boston: Daughters of St. Paul, 1981.

———. Apostolic Exhortation *Redemptoris Custos* [*Guardian of the Redeemer*]. Vatican City State: Libreria Editrice Vaticana, 1989.

Kavunguvalappil, O.C.D., Antony. *Theology of Suffering and the Cross in the Life and Works of Blessed Edith Stein*. European University Studies, vol. 23. Frankfurt am Main: Peter Lang, 1998.

Kölner Selig- und Heiligsprechungsprozess der Dienerin Gottes Sr. Teresia Benedicta a Cruce (Edith Stein): Professe und Chorschwester des Ordens der Allerseligsten Jungfrau Maria vom Berge Karmel. Köln: Kloster der Karmelitinnen Maria vom Frieden, 1962.

Kühn, Rolf. "Leben aus dem Sein: Zur philosophischen Grundin-tuitionen Edith Steins". *Freiburger Zeitschrift für Philosophie und Theologie* 35 (1988): 159–73.

Mechaber, Ezra. "Staying Competitive through Education: The President and American Business Leaders Announce New Commitments". *The White House Blog*. July 18, 2011. http://www.whitehouse.gov/blog/2011/07/18/staying-competitive-through-education-president-and-american-business-leaders-announ.

Oben, Freda Mary. *The Life and Thought of St. Edith Stein*. New York: Alba House, 2001.

Pius XII. Encyclical Letter *Mystici Corporus Christi* [*On the Mystical Body of Christ*]. Vatican City State: Libreria Editrice Vaticana, 1943.

Posselt, Sister Teresia Renata, O.C.D. *Edith Stein: Eine Grosse Frau unseres Jahrhunderts*. 9th ed. Freiburg: Herder, 1963.

———. *Edith Stein: The Life of a Philosopher and Carmelite*. Edited by Susanne M. Batzdorff, Sister Josephine Koeppel, O.C.D., and Reverend John Sullivan, O.C.D. Washing-ton, D.C.: ICS Publications, 2005.

Stein, Edith. *Bildung und Entfaltung der Individualität: Beiträge zum christlichen Erziehungsauftrag.* Edited by Sister Maria Amata Neyer, O.C.D., and Beate Beckmann-Zöller, Freiburg im Breisgau: Herder, 2001. Vol. 16 of *Edith Stein Gesamtausgabe.*

——. *An Edith Stein Daybook: To Live at the Hand of the Lord.* Translated by Susanne M. Batzdorff. Springfield, Ill.: Templegate Publishers, 1994.

——. *Essays on Woman.* 2nd rev. ed. Translated by Freda Mary Oben. Edited by L. Gelber and Romaeus Leuven, O.C.D. Washington, D.C.: ICS Publications, 1996. Vol. 2 of *The Collected Works of Edith Stein.*

——. *Finite and Eternal Being.* Translated by Kurt F. Reinhardt. Edited by L. Gelber and Romaeus Leuven, O.C.D. Washington, D.C.: ICS Publications, 2002. Vol. 9 of *The Collected Works of Edith Stein.*

——. *Ganzheitliches Leben: Schriften zur religiösen Bildung.* Edith Steins Werke, vol. 12. Freiburg: Herder, 1990.

——. *The Hidden Life: Hagiographic Essays, Meditations, Spiritual Texts.* Translated by Waltraut Stein. Edited by L. Gelber and M. Linssen, O.C.D. Washington, D.C.: ICS Publications, 1992. Vol. 6 of *The Collected Works of Edith Stein.*

——. *Life in a Jewish Family (1891–1916).* Translated by Sister Josephine Koeppel, O.C.D. Edited by L. Gelber and Romaeus Leuven, O.C.D. Washington, D.C.: ICS Publications, 1986. Vol. 1 of *The Collected Works of Edith Stein.*

——. *On the Problem of Empathy.* Translated by Waltraut Stein. 3rd ed. Washington, D.C.: ICS Publications, 1989. Vol. 3 of *The Collected Works of Edith Stein.*

——. *Philosophy of Psychology and the Humanities.* Translated by Sister Mary Catharine Baseheart, S.C.N., and Marianne Sawicki. Edited by Marianne Sawicki. Washington, D.C.: ICS Publications, 2000. Vol. 7 of *The Collected Works of Edith Stein.*

————. *The Science of the Cross.* Translated by Sister Josephine Koeppel, O.C.D. Edited by L. Gelber and Romaeus Leuven, O.C.D. Washington, D.C.: ICS Publications, 2002. Vol. 6 of *The Collected Works of Edith Stein.*

————. *Self-Portrait in Letters, 1916–1942.* Translated by Sister Josephine Koeppel, O.C.D. Edited by L. Gelber and Romaeus Leuven, O.C.D. Washington, D.C.: ICS Publications, 1993. Vol. 5 of *The Collected Works of Edith Stein.*

Teresa of Ávila, *The Way of Perfection.* Translated and edited by E. Allison Peers. New York: Image Books, 2004.

von Hildebrand, Alice. *Dietrich von Hildebrand and Edith Stein: Husserl's Students.* Fort Collins, Col.: Roman Catholic Books, 2013.

von Hildebrand, Dietrich. *Christian Ethics.* New York: David McKay Company, Inc., 1953.

INDEX

abstract thought, 63, 77
Adam, 37, 61–62, 140
Advent, 86
angels, 9, 118, 143–44
  the angelic community,
    136–38
anti-Semitism, 71
apostles, 53
apostolate, 31, 84, 151
Aquinas, Saint Thomas, 83
asceticism, ascetical, 69
association, 39n, 119n15
  vs. community, 114–16,
    120–22, 132–34
Atonement, Day of, 26–27,
  35
attitude, 64, 68, 70, 94, 110
  importance of, 127–29
Augustine, Saint, 8
baptism, sacrament of, 10–11,
  25, 32, 39n, 66, 82nn6–7,
  90, 105, 150
  and Mystical Body,
    membership in, 140
beatification and canonization, process of, 66, 83,
  91, 154

Benedict XVI, Pope, 22, 86,
  97n34
Beuron, Benedictine Abbey
  of, 91
Body, Mystical. *See* Mystical
  Body
Bonaventure, Saint, 8
Bouyer, Louis, 20
Breslau University, 27
Breviary, 90
bride, bridal, 10, 64, 87
canonization. *See* beatification
  and canonization, process
  of
career, 9, 58–59, 75–78, 99n2
careerism, 20, 99
Caritas in Veritate, Encyclical
  Letter, 22, 86n14
Carmel, 12, 31–40, 51, 72,
  74, 82, 84, 91, 94n29,
  152–53
carriers of the communal life
  130–32
catechesis, 60
catechism, 29, 66
character, 100, 126, 130, 136
  See also formation